Palestine Explored

PALESTINE EXPLORED.

𝔅𝔞𝔩𝔩𝔞𝔫𝔱𝔶𝔫𝔢 𝔓𝔯𝔢𝔰𝔰

BALLANTYNE, HANSON AND CO.

EDINBURGH AND LONDON

THE SHEPHERD'S CLUB AND STAFF.

See page 255.

PALESTINE EXPLORED

WITH A VIEW TO ITS PRESENT
NATURAL FEATURES, AND TO THE PREVAILING
MANNERS, CUSTOMS, RITES, AND COLLOQUIAL EXPRESSIONS
OF ITS PEOPLE, WHICH THROW LIGHT ON THE
FIGURATIVE LANGUAGE OF THE BIBLE.

BY THE

REV. JAMES NEIL, M.A.

FORMERLY INCUMBENT OF CHRIST CHURCH, JERUSALEM
AUTHOR OF "PALESTINE REPEOPLED," ETC

NEW YORK:
A. D. F. RANDOLPH & CO
900 BROADWAY.
1882.

THE SHEPHERD, DOG, AND STAFF.

PALESTINE EXPLORED

WITH A VIEW TO ITS PRESENT
NATURAL FEATURES, AND TO THE PREVAILING
MANNERS, CUSTOMS, RITES, AND COLLOQUIAL EXPRESSIONS
OF ITS PEOPLE, WHICH THROW LIGHT ON THE
FIGURATIVE LANGUAGE OF THE BIBLE.

BY THE

REV. JAMES NEIL, M.A.

FORMERLY INCUMBENT OF CHRIST CHURCH, JERUSALEM,
AUTHOR OF "PALESTINE REPEOPLED," ETC.

NEW YORK:
A. D. F. RANDOLPH & CO.
900 BROADWAY.
1882.

PREFACE.

THE following pages deal with the author's discoveries in the Holy Land, and those recently made there by others, which throw new light upon the Bible. His chief qualification for the work lies in his having enjoyed an official residence at Jerusalem for three years, from May 1871 to May 1874. During that time he was called upon to traverse Palestine in many directions. The management of landed property in various parts of the country afforded him very special facilities for forming a close acquaintance with its natural features and modern life. Intimate relations with its various races, and more particularly with native Jews, amongst whom Hebrew is still a spoken language, gave further help. Nor must the advantage derived from the invaluable aid of the Palestine Exploration Fund be overlooked. The greater part of the Ordnance Survey of Western Palestine, which, to the Biblical student, is by far the most important scientific work of this scientific age, was accomplished during the period of the author's residence at Jerusalem, and he has watched its progress throughout.

It was not until his return to England that the force and bearing of many observations were fully realised. A second visit to the East was made in February 1875. Three months were then occupied by a journey up the Nile throughout the length of Egypt, and in once more traversing the Land of Israel. This opportunity served to test carefully many conclusions, and to widen a former experience.

The various excellent volumes which have hitherto appeared on this subject deal with Scripture allusions in general. As far as the author is aware, this is the first attempt to treat in an original manner of Palestine life as it bears upon those allusions only which occur by way of figurative language.

Frequent glances at Hebrew philology, or the study of the precise meaning of Hebrew words, could not be avoided. Its claims, in our day, no student of the Word, however humble, can afford to forget. It is not less true that no intelligent layman, albeit unacquainted with a single letter of the ancient language of Canaan, need doubt for a moment his full capacity to enter with intense interest and no little profit into many simple branches of this important study.

The reader will find that all passages which occur

as poetry in the Hebrew Scriptures are uniformly
given in this work in the form of poetical extracts.
He will also find that all the numerous quotations
from both the Old and New Testaments are carefully retranslated, wherever the adoption of a more
authentic reading of the text, the employment of a
more accurate rendering of it, or the excision of the
obsolete words or grammatical constructions which
occur in our version have called for an improve-
ment. This has sprung from a twofold purpose—
first, to give in each case, as truthfully as possible,
the very language of inspiration; and secondly, to
prepare the minds of all for the new revised version
of the Bible now appearing, which, right and necessary as it is, can scarcely fail to prove a shock to
some pious people who have not read the Word of
God in the original.

The attention of those who are charged with the
deeply responsible duty of making the revision of
the Old Testament is respectfully but earnestly
invited to some important renderings suggested in
this work. Some of these are drawn from the
terms for common objects which the writer found
in constant use in all parts of the country. Where
the modern colloquial Arabic spoken in Palestine,
by a people who are now held to be a remnant
of the original Canaanitish nations, retains, as it so
often does, the very same word which we find in

the Hebrew Scriptures employed in a similar connection, with a precise technical meaning—a meaning which can be consistently and naturally applied
to all, or almost all, the passages where it occurs,
and which, when so applied, gives a new appropriateness and beauty to each—can we doubt that
this is the true and accurate meaning which the
Spirit of God intended to convey ?

The indulgent reception given to the author's
former work on the present of Palestine in relation
to its future, which has now almost run through its
seventh edition, has encouraged him to put forth this
view of its present in relation to its past. May He
who bade us "search the Scriptures" be revealed to
all who peruse these pages. They have been written
throughout to the praise of His name.

Olicana House, Ilkley, Yorkshire,
    September 1881.

CONTENTS.

ILLUSTRATIONS.

PALESTINE EXPLORED.

CHAPTER I.

THE BIBLE IN PALESTINE.

"Why do they on the Sabbath-day that which is not lawful?"[1] said the Pharisees to Christ with reference to an act of His disciples. To the mind of the author in childhood the case afforded a still graver difficulty. "Why do they that which is not lawful upon *any* day?" was the anxious inquiry that haunted him, though he did not dare to express it openly. The Master with His humble followers had been passing through fields of ripening corn. These poor hungry men, seeing the golden ears gleaming amid their beards of black awns, had plucked them off, and rubbing out the grain between their palms, had satisfied with this simple fare the cravings of appetite. In fact, it seems that the whole company had made there and then a full repast. Now, in every

---

[1] Mark ii. 24.

A

part of our country a much less offence than this, even the plucking of a single ear, would be a misdemeanour to be punished by the magistrate, and that sometimes very severely. The act of our Saviour's followers, measured by the only standard of which he knew, amounted to wilful theft. Great was the perplexity caused by a consideration of the whole narrative, and great was his gladness in after years to be permitted to enjoy repeated opportunities of realising the strict regularity of the whole proceeding during his residence in the Holy Land.

There the right of a traveller to pluck and eat his fill of wheat, or even to allow his horse to browse in passing on the standing crop of barley, is a part of the time-honoured common law of those truly hospitable regions. The tillage, lying for miles in one unbroken stretch with no walls, hedges, or ditches, renders this privilege both easy and natural, without involving any trespass. Wheat and barley in Syria present few of the difficulties experienced in their culture in more northern lands. Palestine, next to Egypt, is the very home of these grains. Every rocky patch on the hill slopes, which with us would only be accounted a goat pasture, is there sown broadcast, and in favourable seasons makes an astonishingly bountiful return. Hence the unprotected position of arable ground rendering prohibition difficult, if not impossible, together with the proverbial abundance of the crops, have jointly contributed to establish this charitable custom from the earliest times.

It is, of course, perfectly true that a close acquaintance with Scripture would have entirely reconciled the author's youthful difficulty, short of his Syrian experience, for this charter of the stranger and the poor was incorporated in the law of Moses. In that statute-book of Palestine we read, " When thou comest into the standing corn of thy neighbour, then thou mayest pluck the ears with thine hand; but thou shalt not move a sickle unto thy neighbour's standing corn." [1] But it is placed here as one of very many serious difficulties which all have felt some time or other in reading the Bible, as a natural consequence of its Oriental and exotic features. These difficulties are none the less great because, as in this instance, through a false sense of reverence, they sometimes remain unspoken, and often, contrary to the case in question, could not possibly be explained by any mere comparison with other inspired passages.

The Bible is as much an Eastern book as the " Arabian Nights' Entertainment." It is usual to

---

[1] Deuteronomy xxiii. 25. In the previous verse permission is given to eat " thy fill of grapes at thine own pleasure " when passing through a neighbouring vineyard, so long as none are put into a vessel to be carried away. This, too, is still a recognised custom in Palestine.

speak of the Scriptures as the simplest and plainest
of works. In one sense this is beautifully true.
Man's ruin, redemption, renewal to holiness, and
resurrection glory with Christ Jesus, are reiterated
again and again, so clearly that the inquiring soul,
taught by the Spirit, cannot err as to these essential
doctrines. Yet they are frequently illustrated and
enforced by figurative language embodying facts,
ideas, and phrases wholly foreign to our daily experience. Thus the honest and thoughtful reader finds
himself constantly coming upon passages that appear
unintelligible. In a word, the very thoughts and
expressions employed by the inspired writers to
render the subject more lucid are themselves found
to present new and formidable difficulties! And
the reason for this is plain. The traveller who, for
the first time, visits the East—the land and home
of the Bible—finds himself in a new world. It is
not too much to say that almost everything which
surrounds us in England differs from the present life
of Palestine, a life which bears on its simple features
the stamp of a hoary antiquity. This is the full and
simple explanation.

It is not that Moses, or David, or Isaiah, or the
Lord Christ made reference to any abstruse or
unusual matters. Quite the reverse. They drew
their countless allusions from everyday familiar
objects of the very simplest kind, far simpler, as I

hope to show in the following pages, than many have supposed. They wrote for the masses. It was the purpose of the Eternal Spirit to make revelation exceedingly plain. But we are apt to overlook the significant fact that the Bible was written by Easterns, in the East, and for Easterns. Indeed, a great part of it was written exclusively for the use of Easterns for many ages. The very matters, therefore, which made the sacred volume clear to those to whom it was first addressed, make it in just the same proportion obscure to us.

The references to Oriental affairs which we meet with in narrative passages are often, by the help of the context, rendered comparatively plain. The largest number of allusions to be met with in Scripture, however, occur as figures of speech, and as such are necessarily far less easy to be understood.

Next to a sublime simplicity, which is without a rival in any writing, and an emphatic repetition of ideas and phrases, which has been far too little admired and imitated, nothing perhaps is more characteristic of Holy Scripture, viewed as a literary work, than its boundless exuberance of highly figurative language. The Spirit of God, who ever works with men from their own natural standpoint, speaking through the children of the East as the chosen instruments of revelation, has breathed upon the rich imagination of the Orient, and consecrated all

its inimitable imagery to the service of Jehovah.
It is on this account that I have confined my researches to those manners, customs, natural features,
and expressions which are referred to in figurative
language.

We live in sadly sceptical times.   Yet let it be
remembered that, in too many instances, the abstract
and unreal treatment of sacred subjects has paved
the way to the present popular worship of doubt
and uncertainty.   An excellent method of dealing
with the epidemic of modern unbelief is to make
much of the realistic elements of the Bible.   This
healthy study meets Materialism upon its own
ground.   The living identity and reality of the
various subjects alluded to in the Bible should now
be set before intelligent men.   They should be invited to consider the simple fact that the most
ancient book the world can show, and the ruined
land concerning which most of it speaks, answer to
one another like the two parts of an indenture.
They should be shown that the very difficulties
and anomalies which that book at first sight pre-
sents are only so many convincing incidental proofs
of its being, at least from a literary standpoint, just
what it claims to be; nay more, that *if these grave
surface difficulties were absent, the book could not
possibly be genuine !*

To take an example of the singular force of this

argument, let us consider for a moment the highly damaging objection sometimes urged against Holy Scripture on the ground of the coarseness of the expressions it contains, and the handling of subjects the very mention of which we should account impure. I know that this has been an honest difficulty to many earnest and sensitive minds. Yet a comparatively short residence in Palestine serves to remove it altogether; and indeed no Eastern could possibly see any objection whatever on this score. They still, as in ancient times, use the greatest plainness of speech throughout the Holy Land. At first a Western sense of delicacy is greatly shocked. Things, the very mention of which decency forbids amongst us, are there spoken of freely before women and children by people of the highest class, and of the greatest respectability and refinement. As soon as one acquires a knowledge of Arabic, which is virtually but a softer and more copious form of Hebrew, the ear is assailed by a plain-speaking on these subjects which is extremely embarrassing until such time as one becomes accustomed to it. This explains, however, at once the perfect naturalness and innocency of the use of expressions and the mention of matters which our translators have softened down in some instances, and public readers have tacitly agreed to omit in others. Nay more, I will go further and boldly say, that seeing the

Bible purports to be an Eastern book, written in the East, and first—and for long ages only—addressed to Easterns, it could not possibly be genuine if these very matters, which have given rise to such blasphemous cavils, were absent from its pages !

Again, let us glance at an Old Testament narrative, which has caused as much of anxiety and perplexity to sincere believers as of encouragement and triumph to the enemies of the truth.   We read that Sisera, after his sudden defeat on the east of the plain of Esdraelon, fled away to the tent of Jael, the wife of Heber the Kenite.   As he made towards the now deserted encampment, where she appears to have been left alone, she came out and invited him to enter, and then presented him with "a lordly dish" of milk, that is, the ordinary wooden bowl of the country, almost as large as a hand-basin, containing *lĕbĕn*, or goat's sour buttermilk, the only milk an Arab drinks.   As soon, however, as he had sunk into a deep sleep, she took a "nail of the tent," one of the sharp tent-pegs, made of exceedingly hard wood, and a "hammer," or huge wooden mallet, employed to drive these pegs into the ground, both of which are still in use, and slew Sisera by driving the tent-peg through his temples.[1]

---

[1] Judges iv. 17–21. The Hebrew word for "nail" is יָתֵד, *yathaid*, or as it may be *yataid*, and the precisely similar word in Arabic, allowing for the rules of transliteration, *wataid*, is the modern

Now, even sound evangelical commentators have
not hesitated to denounce this act as one of cruel
treachery and deliberate murder. Viewed in the
light of Bible lands, the crime would be tenfold
more heinous and unnatural. Amongst the nomad
tribes of Palestine and the surrounding deserts the
rites of hospitality are peculiarly sacred and inviol-
able. Base beyond description would that wretch
be accounted who, having first entertained a stranger,
not to say an ally, in " a house of hair," [1] afterwards
took his life when he laid down to rest. Yet in the
very next chapter the prophetess Deborah, in a grand
inspired song, prefaces a recital of this incident with
words of the highest commendation—

> " Blessed among women be Jael,
>   The wife of Heber the Kenite,
>   Blessed let her be among women in the tent." [2]

How can the difficulty be reconciled—a difficulty
which has caused the most painful disquietude to
countless tender consciences ? The answer is quite
plain, for in Palestine a perfectly natural and satisfactory explanation at once appears. Jael, left alone
by herself, separated from her husband and his servants, who appear to have been at a distance with

technical term for the wooden tent-pegs about a foot and a half long,
used for driving into the ground to form attachments for the cords
by which the goat's-hair tents are stretched and held in position.

[1] The Arab name for a tent.　　　　[2] Judges v. 24.

the flocks, sees the general of Jabin's forces running
towards her tent, determined to force an entrance.
What could she do to resist an armed and desperate
man? No other course was possible save to do as
we read she did, namely, put a good face on the
matter, and ask him in. But the point on which the
narrative turns is this. Sisera had no right to enter
her tent at all. The women's apartment of an Arab
tent, the only place in it where any privacy exists,
must never, under any circumstances, be entered by
a man. Instances are recorded amongst the Arabs
of a defeated warrior having hidden himself in the
apartments of women; but such a heinous breach
of Eastern etiquette has in each case been followed
by the sentence of death. The insult and wrong
done to Jael from the point of view of a *Bedaween*
woman was such that, in order to avenge her honour,
her husband or her brother would have been bound
by the unwritten but inflexible code of Eastern law
to take Sisera's life. She simply became the execu-
tioner of a sentence which some other person would,
under ordinary circumstances, have carried out. This
alters the whole case; and Jael, instead of being a
cruel, lawless, treacherous creature, becomes, from
the only standard by which we have any right to
judge her, a true heroine. It is most interesting to
observe that in Deborah's inspired commendation
of the conduct of Heber's wife, particular stress is

laid upon the fact of her being a *Bedaween* woman,
and acting nobly and righteously from a *Bedaween's*
point of view—

"Blesséd let her be *among women in the tent.*"

This could not possibly have been said if it were a case
of treachery or murder in connection with a guest.

There is another fact connected with camp life
in Palestine that came under my own personal
observation, which strengthens the presumption
that, in asking Sisera to enter the tent, Jael, thrown
suddenly into a position of great peril, was only
acting throughout under the pressure of fear and
necessity, and was from the first solely intent upon
defending herself and her reputation by tactics
which any Arab woman would consider lawful.
We are specially told that she went out of her
way to offer him *lĕbĕn,* or curdled milk. This act
receives strong emphasis in the poetical version of
the story: and not without reason. *Lĕbĕn* is that
delightful preparation of goat's-milk largely drunk
in Palestine amongst the pastoral tribes. It is
goat's-milk with the butter left in it made sour,
or curdled, by an artificial process. No more excellent, wholesome, or medicinal drink is to be
found in a hot country. It possesses in particular
one peculiar and invaluable property. It has a
remarkably soothing anti-feverish effect on the

nervous system when disordered by fatigue, and
acts as a strong soporific. I have myself experienced the pleasant sleep-inducing effects of this
beverage. On one occasion, when suffering from
much sleeplessness and nervous excitement brought
on by great fatigue, I partook of it very freely at a
Bedaween camp on the north of the plain of Sharon.
So strong was its action that, after resting for half
an hour, I could only with the greatest difficulty
continue my journey, in consequence of the drowsi-
ness that came over me. Indeed, my first impres-
sion was that the draught must have been drugged,
so sudden and powerful were its narcotic effects.
There can be little doubt that Jael's purpose in
supplying *lĕbĕn* so liberally to Sisera was to send
him into a sound and deep sleep. If so, then her
conduct throughout appears to have been perfectly
consistent as an attempt to punish in a summary
but lawful way, what in her eyes, and the eyes of
her people, was an unpardonable crime, committed
by a well-known and unscrupulous tyrant who seems
to have trusted for impunity to his high rank.[1]

Once more, the great and to us unnatural frequency with which references to weapons of war
occur in the Hebrew prophets must have struck all
careful readers of the Bible. I was on one occasion

---

[1] I am indebted for the idea of the above explanation to Lieutenant Conder's *Tent Work in Palestine*, vol. i. p. 133.

at considerable pains to draw up a complete view of the different sources from which the various images employed in the Psalms are derived. I found, upon classifying every figure of speech which occurs in this book under its own proper subject heading that out of the fourteen subjects into which all the illustrations could be naturally divided, weapons of war came third in order of frequency. Such a fact supplies in itself a forcible undesigned coincidence which may be viewed as a strong proof of the genuineness of this grand Prayer-book and Hymn-book of the Universal Church. To the present day in Palestine almost every man, however quiet his occupation or disposition, goes about armed, and while travelling is often armed to the teeth. The bow and arrows of Bible times, and with them the shield, have now given place to a very old-fashioned gun, with the use of which all the male population are perfectly familiar; and indeed most Syrian peasants, if allowed an artificial rest for their long, clumsy fire-arms, command a very deadly aim. The stout heavy-headed wooden club, the dagger, or knife, and the sling are everywhere to be seen at the present day, and so, though less frequently, are the " club of iron," or formidable spiked iron mace, and the spear, or javelin, these latter mostly carried by *Derweeshes*. The sword, too, is now a common weapon amongst all classes of civilians, and one they know well how to wield. Endless family feuds, border warfare, *Bedaween* raids, and desperate attacks by robbers, still as of old call these weapons constantly into use; and so also do the ravages of the wild beasts which infest most of the highways. The universal practice in this matter amongst the people at large adds a very special force, and one that we should naturally overlook, to the wretched state of bondage under which Israel must have lain in the days of Saul, when they were so thoroughly disarmed by the Philistines that " there was neither sword nor spear found in the hand of any of the people." [1]

Upon first landing in Palestine, I determined that I would not carry weapons, regarding them as inconsistent with my peaceful calling. I had not, however, resided there many months, during which long journeys had to be made alone by night, before I discovered that it was, humanly speaking, absolutely necessary to bear fire-arms, as all around me were doing, if only as a protection against the wild animals that roam about after dark. Upon reflecting on the course of action I was thus most unwillingly led to adopt, I perceived a practical and perfectly satisfactory explanation of our Lord's words, which have proved a source of such trouble to sensitive souls, and of such serious censure on

[1] 1 Samuel xiii. 19-22.

the part of objectors. In one of His last discourses
the Saviour announced to His disciples that, after
His death, they would no longer be sent out as
formerly, but that, in taking their missionary journeys, they were henceforth to make the ordinary,
lawful, and necessary provisions for travelling. He
said, "'When I sent you forth without purse, and
leathern bag, and shoes, lacked ye anything?' and
they said, 'Nothing.' Then He said unto them: 'But
now, he that hath a purse, let him take it, and likewise a leathern bag, and *he that hath none, let him sell
his cloak, and buy a sword.* ... And they said: 'Lord,
behold, *here are two swords.' And He said unto them,
'It is enough.'*"[1] I learnt by the experience of
everyday life that these words, in their fullest
meaning, implied no more than saying, "Take now
the usual precautions which all prudent and experienced people employ when setting out upon long
and dangerous journeys." No Syrian could fail for
a moment to understand the Master's meaning, or
the absolute necessity for such an injunction, unless
Christians were to be preserved by a perpetual
miracle. Many similar examples might be adduced
to show how a great number of the cavils of unbelievers arise really from ignorance, and cannot live
for a moment in the light of a thorough knowledge
of Palestine life.

[1] Luke xxii. 35, 36, 38.

There is a consideration, to which we are strangers in these highly civilised lands of the West, that lends a great and peculiar importance to researches in the Land of Israel. I allude to the marvellous uniformity and antiquity of the present manners and customs and artificial productions throughout this and the surrounding countries. The origin of most of their customs is so ancient as to be lost in remote ages. All that members of the oldest families can say, when asked to account for the present habits of the people, is " Our fathers did thus ; " " It is from ancient times ; " " It always was done so." Notwithstanding the numerous races and religions which have for centuries swept in turn across these ruined regions, there remains a stereotyped agreement in almost all the common affairs of life. If we speak of a plough, then from the south of Egypt to the far north of Syria, on every farm this implement is of precisely the same make. In every house you visit the little handleless cup out of which you sip your coffee is of the same size and pattern, and so are the basin and ewer with which the servant of your host, when he has girded himself and taken a towel, washes your hands. In each class of life both men and women respectively dress alike, and strange as it sounds to us, the material, colour, and style of apparel in the rural districts are wholly unaffected by any new modes, but in the memory of man have continued in all respects precisely the same! No changing fashions, no progress in arts or science varies, or ever appears to have varied, the simple appliances of Palestine. The state of the country, viewed in this light, is a standing miracle.

The language, too, which is now in use retains in all respects the very phrases of Scripture. Still the only names by which the days of the week are known are the same as of old. The Lord's-day is "the first day of the week," Monday is "the second day," and so on with the rest.[1] Still the day is said to begin at sunset, and is reckoned, as in the very first chapter of Genesis, from the evening to the morning.[2] Still the hours of the day are the same; the first of the night being an hour after sunset, and the eleventh hour of the night an hour before sunrise; the first hour of the day being the first after sunrise, and the eleventh hour of the day an hour before sunset.[3] Still all distances are computed not by miles, but by the hours or days which

[1] Genesis i. 5, 8, 13, 19, 23, 31 ; ii. 2, &c.
[2] Genesis i. 5, &c. ; Exodus xxvii. 21 ; Psalm lv. 17, &c.
[3] Mark xv. 25 ; Matthew xxvii. 46 ; John iv. 52 ; Acts xxiii. 23. At the equinoxes the first hour of the day is six o'clock A.M., and the first hour of the night six o'clock P.M. The third hour then answers to our nine o'clock A.M. Though there is a difference in the length of the days in summer and winter, it is not in the latitude of Palestine nearly so great as with us. It does not much exceed four hours between the longest and shortest days. The day is

B

it takes to accomplish them.[1]   The very names
of most of the villages and ruins, and we have
now ten thousand names on the Survey Map of
Western Palestine, have a meaning in Hebrew.[2]   Do
you desire, like Abraham, to make a purchase, the
seller still says, in the words of Ephron the Hittite,
"My Lord, . . . I give it thee."[3]   One not related
by blood, but whom it is desired to honour, and
sometimes a complete stranger, is addressed like
Elisha as "my father,"[4] or like Jonathan as "my
brother."[5]   The common salutation, like that of
Joseph's steward, is "peace be unto thee;"[6] and the
honoured guest is bid to enter as of yore with the
words that greeted Abraham's servant, "Come in,
thou blessed of the Lord."[7]   Still, if a man con-
firms a matter with an oath, he cries, "As God
liveth," or "As the Lord liveth."[8]   Does he seek
to reassure you, or to protest his uprightness, he
says with Joseph, "I fear God."[9]   A farmer coming

always considered as divided into twelve hours (John xi. 9), and
these hours are shorter in winter and longer in summer.   Noon is
a fixed *period*, much used by Easterns in reckoning time (Genesis
xliii. 16 ; Judges xix. 8 ; 2 Samuel iv. 5 ; 1 Kings xviii. 26, &c.),
though not a fixed *hour ;* but sunset is always twelve o'clock.

[1] Genesis xxx. 36, xxxi. 23 ; 1 Kings xix. 4.
[2] *Tent Life in Palestine.*   By Lieut. C. R. Conder, R.E., vol.
i. p. 375.
[3] Genesis xxiii. 11.   [4] 2 Kings ii. 12, vi. 21.   [5] 2 Samuel i. 26.
[6] Genesis xliii. 23 ; Judges vi. 23, &c.   [7] Genesis xxiv. 31.
[8] 2 Samuel ii. 27 ; Jeremiah iv. 2.   [9] Genesis xlii. 18.

into his fields to this day will greet his labourers in the very words of Boaz, "The Lord be with you," and will receive for answer, "The Lord bless thee." [1] Indeed, there is scarcely a devout expression to be found in the pages of Holy Writ that does not now flow, alas! but too insincerely, from the tongue of modern dwellers in Palestine. Does a sheikh, or chief, desire in an emergency to assemble his allies for war, he does so with the cry of Jehu, "Who is on my side? Who?" [2] Evening is still called as it was four thousand years ago, "the time that women go out to draw water." [3] If you meet them by the well, and request them to give you a draught, like Rebekah of old, they will let down their pitcher upon their hand, and say, "Drink, my Lord." [4] If you ask them where any principal resident of their village is to be found, should he be at home, you will still receive the same answer as Saul and his servant, "Behold, he is before you." [5] The poor, ignorant, oppressed peasant, to whom the writings of Jeremiah and Ezekiel are all unknown, nevertheless, in the very language of inspiration, wearily asks the English traveller when his nation are coming "to build up the land again." [6] In a word, to this day, in things sacred and secular, the speech of all Syria is unchanged, and listening to it one

[1] Ruth ii. 4. [2] 2 Kings ix. 32. [3] Genesis xxiv. 11. [4] Genesis xxiv. 18
[5] 1 Samuel ix. 12. [6] Jeremiah xviii. 9 ; Ezekiel xxxvi. 10.

catches everywhere distinct and startling echoes of Scripture story.

Well has it been said, " Immutability is the most striking law of Eastern life." This unchangeableness gives immense weight to all researches into the present condition of Palestine. We have had of late much very important work done by the Palestine Exploration Fund. The *land* has been surveyed throughout by able men with most valuable and interesting results. But far more interesting and valuable discoveries are to be made in an exploration of its *life*. Not only are many questions of topography of comparatively minor value to the Biblical student, even when perfectly clear, but such is the state of emptiness, ignorance, wasting, and generally decay into which the country has fallen for upwards of a thousand years that a perfect identification of most Scriptural sites is scarcely possible. But in the case of the manners, customs, productions, great natural features, and a large part of the language of the people, these through ages of convulsion have survived unaltered, and may be seen and heard to-day in Emmanuel's Land the same in all essentials as they were seen and heard by David three thousand years ago. Ruin has been able to make but little havoc in these living, divinely-preserved commentaries on the Written Word. And more than this, the simple, everyday features of

Palestine life, when once recognised, throw, in very many instances, a broad flood of light across the pages of the Bible. The identification of the site of a city may serve to explain one or two important narratives, but the discovery of an ancient custom, a regular atmospherical phenomenon, or a technical expression still on the lips of the people, may give a new force—ay, perhaps a new meaning—to a hundred passages. That this is really the case I trust to show in many parts of the following pages.

CHAPTER II.

MISCELLANEOUS ILLUSTRATIONS.

"I use similitudes by the ministry of the prophets."
—HOSEA xii. 10.

A VERY familiar feature of Eastern life meets the traveller as he enters Palestine. Upon his first stepping ashore at Jaffa, the ancient Joppa, he sees around the landing stage a shouting, struggling crowd of porters. These men, whose occupation is known in Arabic as that of the *'atal,* or *hammal,* contend frantically for his belongings, which one of their number finally carries away upon his back to the traveller's hotel. Such *'atals* find regular employment in all the towns, for the absence of carts renders their services constantly necessary. They are generally clad in a coarse, almost indestructible tunic of camel's-hair cloth. Their sole stock-in-trade is a stout rope about five yards long.

The weights that these men will lift, and under which they will stagger along for a considerable distance, are truly amazing. Immense packing-cases, full of heavy articles, sacks of wheat and other produce, or large pieces of furniture, as the case may be, are first piled up together. The 'atal, or porter, then crouches down with his back against the heaped-up articles which are to form his load, and having skilfully arranged his rope without any knots so as to catch and sustain them all, and taking one end of it in each hand, with a sudden spring rises to his feet, and brings the whole weight to bear upon his shoulders and the upper part of his back. In this effort to rise, they have a habit of emptying their lungs by the expiration of breath in a loud kind of grunt. Men amongst ourselves engaged in very heavy lifting labour make just the same noise when in the act of putting their system to an unusually violent strain. But for the relief afforded by this sudden expiration they would be in imminent danger of rupturing a blood-vessel. I have often gazed at these poor fellows with mingled wonder and pity, as I have seen them staggering past me along the broken and slippery stone paths of the streets in Jerusalem, bowed down under burdens so huge in bulk and heavy in weight as to seem altogether beyond human strength. Certainly no class of men in any country earn a harder livelihood, or are exposed to a severer strain. Were not the physical powers of these Syrian peasants, where patient endurance is in question, developed in a very remarkable degree, they could not engage all day long in such work.

It would seem that the reference to grievous distresses under the figure of "burdens," so frequently occurring in the poetical portions of Scripture, receives much force from a consideration of the above facts. Moses complains to God, "Thou layest the burden of all this people upon me," in allusion to the crushing weight of responsibility involved in conducting the helpless and thankless crowds of Israel through the desert of Sinai, before his labours were lightened by the appointment of seventy elders.[1]

David says in his anguish of soul—

> "Mine iniquities are gone over my head,
>   As a heavy burden, they are too heavy for me."[2]

Constantly have I seen the porter's huge load reaching far over and above his head, which he has had to hold down on this account in a bowed and painful position. It was probably from this text that the "glorious dreamer" took the idea which he has embodied in the first scenes of his *Pilgrim's Progress*. All the illustrations that I have noticed of this subject set forth Christian at the beginning of his way as bearing on his back a good-sized bundle, such as might be carried by a strong man with

[1] Numbers xi. 11, 25.   [2] Psalm xxxviii. 4.

comparative ease. Very different was the familiar
picture that rose before David when he thought of
a wearied soul burdened beyond measure by a deep
conviction of sin, a picture no doubt such as I have
attempted to describe, and which was daily to be
witnessed from his palace windows.   I would com-
mend it to the notice of any who may in future
illustrate Bunyan's allegory.   And here let me say,
in passing, that the highly conventional and unreal
character of most of the pictures to be met with in
books of Scriptural scenes and Scriptural subjects
is much to be deplored.   A well and truthfully
illustrated Bible is a great want of the age.   Doré,
whose work in this respect has been so much
admired, is full of inaccuracies.   For instance, in
the meeting of Isaac and Rebekah, he represents
the bride in the act of stepping off her camel while
it remains standing, in entire ignorance of the fact
that at mounting or descending this tall quadruped
is always made to kneel down !

In the prophets the " burden " is used as a most
expressive metaphor to set forth the denunciation of
heavy judgments.[1]   Our Blessed Lord, too, has a
plain reference to the toil of the 'atal when, speaking
of the cruelly oppressive ceremonial traditions forced

[1] Isaiah xiii. 1; xv. 1; xvii. 1; xix. 1; xxiii. 1; xxx. 6; Jeremiah
xxiii. 33, 34, 36, 38 ; Lamentations ii. 14; Ezekiel xii. 10; Hosea
viii. 10 ; Nahum i. 1 ; Habakkuk i. 1, &c.

upon the people by the hypocritical Scribes and
Pharisees, He tells us that these spiritual taskmasters " bind heavy burdens and grievous to
be borne, and lay them on men's shoulders; but
they themselves will not move them with their
finger." [1]   In beautiful contrast to such wearisome
ritualistic and ceremonial observances, that only
tend to bondage and oppression, Jesus emphatically
declares, " My burden is light." [2]

A picturesque and evidently ancient custom
is still lingering in the chief cities of Egypt,
and forms one of the many strange contrasts
of ancient and modern civilisation to be witnessed in the land of the Pharaohs.   When people
of wealth or position drive abroad in the European
carriages which have taken the place of the cum-
brous chariots of former days, they are preceded by
an attendant, who is called a *sais*, or groom, and
whose duty it is to run on foot at some distance in
advance of the carriage.   As almost every office or
service throughout the East is distinguished by its
own peculiar costume, these men are all habited
alike.   Their dress is peculiarly light and picturesque.   The feet and lower part of the legs are
bare.   Their spotlessly white tunic has large, flowing, fanshaped sleeves, which as they begin to run,

[1] Matthew xxiii. 4.   [2] Matthew xi. 30.

holding their arms stretched out, appear like wings. This tunic is gathered in by a scarf round the waist, and above it they wear a short, sleeveless, velvet jacket profusely embroidered with gold or silver lace; and in their hands they carry a long light wand.

Their office is to clear the way before their master's equipage, to open gates, to announce his coming, and to wait upon him when the carriage halts. They use their wands freely on all who occupy the road and do not at once withdraw, often breaking them over the shoulders of those who pay no heed to their warning cry. Their speed, strength, and powers of endurance are remarkable. People drive at a very rapid rate in Cairo. Those who have walked through its narrow streets have experienced the great risk of injury to which foot-passengers are exposed on this account. Yet an Egyptian *sais* will run, without stopping, before his master's carriage driven thus swiftly for a distance of twelve miles! The Viceroy only allows a subject, however great his rank, to be attended by one *sais*, and the equipages of the royal family are always known by the accompaniment of two such grooms or out-runners. These attendants also go with their employers when they ride on horseback. A similar custom exists, as travellers tell us, in the chief cities of Persia. That it should have almost died out in

Palestine itself and most of the surrounding districts is fully accounted for by the want of settled government, the general poverty which prevails in these parts, and the ruined state of the roads, which entirely precludes the use of any wheeled vehicle.

The modern *sais* of Egypt appears to perform the part of the "runner," or "footman," frequently referred to in the Bible as attached to the household of kings and nobles. When Samuel warned the people of "the manner of the king" that they so eagerly desired to reign over them, amongst other hard services that the monarch would exact, he enumerated this, and put it at the head of a long list, as one of the most laborious and oppressive. "Your sons he will take and appoint for himself, for his chariots and his horsemen; and they shall run before his chariots." [1] We read that when Absalom began to conspire against his father and to assume royal honours, he "prepared for himself chariots and horses, and fifty men to run before him." [2] When some eight years afterwards Adonijah, the son of Haggith, "exalted himself, saying, 'I will be king,'" he did precisely the same thing. [3] These facts lend great force to the act of Elijah, who in an ecstasy of joy and zeal at the triumph of Jehovah, and desirous to "honour the king" who for a brief moment had honoured God, when the hand of the

[1] Samuel viii. 11.   [2] 2 Samuel xv. 1.   [3] 1 Kings i. 5.

Lord came upon him, " girded up his loins, and ran before Ahab to the entrance of Jezreel," [1]—that is, for a distance of some twenty miles or more across the great plain of Esdraelon the man of God acted as the *sais* or runner of the king, clearing a way for his chariot and announcing his arrival! Possibly, from the haste with which the king started on his unforeseen journey, urged by Elijah, none of the royal outrunners were at hand or in readiness to attend upon their master; and viewed in this light the act of the prophet, though not the less miraculous, appears the more natural, loyal, and chivalrous.

Would not this office of the outrunner appear to furnish the graphic and forcible allusion of the Apostle Paul in the conclusion of the passage where he speaks of that hope in Christ which is the sheet-anchor of the soul? Describing this hope as an anchor thrown on high " which entereth into the part within the veil," that is, the spot typified by the Holy of Holies, heaven itself, he adds, with that sudden change of figure which is so characteristic of his terse and vigorous style, " whither Jesus entered for us as a forerunner." [2] What a depth of meaning is here! He who came " not to be ministered unto, but to minister," and who condescended to be among His people on earth " as one who serveth," seems to Paul like the " runner," who just

---

[1] 1 Kings xviii. 44-46.   [2] Hebrews vi. 20.

precedes by a little the chariot of the prince to prepare his way, and to enter into the gates of the
palace and take possession in his name. His people,
whom He has Himself declared are to be "kings"
unto God, and of whom He has said that, even when
He is in heaven, verily "He will gird Himself, and
make them to sit down to meat, and will come forth
and serve them," are represented, for "their strong
consolation," as themselves already taking possession
in Jesus of the Father's House. He as their outrunner is pictured by the Apostle as having entered
in only a brief moment earlier to appear in heaven
for them, to announce their arrival, and to be prepared to receive and wait upon them there! Thus
is it ever with Him, our merciful Saviour, who, because He is God, lives to serve and succour those
of His faithful creatures who are the work of His
hands, the redeemed of His blood, and the joy of
His heart, and Who has repeatedly condescended to
set forth the nature of that service He so tenderly
affords them under figures of the lowliest offices.

One of the characteristic sights of Palestine,
shortly after the harvest has been gathered in, is
the measuring out of wheat and barley, which sometimes takes place in the corn-market, but more
frequently in the courtyard of the purchaser's house.
All families at this time, that is during July and

August, lay up in store the wheat which will be required to provide bread for the use of the household throughout the ensuing year, and also barley sufficient for their horses, mules, and asses during the same period. Samples are procured either from the farmer or merchant, and when approved the whole quantity ordered is delivered to the purchaser bound up in sacks. A professional measurer is always present on these occasions, and in the presence of the seller and buyer, or their representatives, duly proceeds to ascertain the contents of each sack. This is done by meting out the grain in a circular wooden measure in the shape of our own bushel measure, but less deep, called in Arabic a *timneh*. The measurer seats himself cross-legged on the ground, and proceeds to shovel the wheat or barley, as the case may be, into the *timneh* with both his hands until it is partly full. Next he seizes the measure, and shakes it strongly from side to side, by means of two or three rapid half turns without raising it from the ground, in order that the grain may settle into a smaller space. This quick shaking together of the corn is a striking part of the process, and is very effective in forcing it to occupy less room. He then fills it further, and repeats the shaking from side to side, going over the same thing again and again until it is full up to the brim. As soon as this is the case, he gently but firmly presses

upon it with his hands, so as to drive it into a yet
smaller space. Finally, having first made a slight
hollow on the top, he takes some more handfuls of
grain, and very skilfully constructs a cone of corn
upon the flat surface of the *timneh*, which he has
now filled. He continues carefully to build up this
cone until no more grain can possibly be held, and
that which he adds begins to flow over and run
down. Upon this the measure is considered to be
of full weight, and is emptied into the purchaser's
sack. This is the universal method by which grain
is now meted out, and the price is always quoted at
so much per *timneh*.

These professional measurers are often dishonest,
taking bribes from seller or buyer, and in this case
are very skilful in cheating either party as it suits
their purpose. If it is to their interest to do so,
while apparently going through the ordinary process,
they can so contrive as to bring the contents of the
measure to half a *rottle*, or three pounds, less than
the proper quantity, involving a loss to the purchaser
of over six per cent. On the other hand, their dis-
honesty more commonly favours the merchants and
townspeople, who buy from the poor *fellahheen*, the
peasants. The cunning of the measurers in this
way is said to be brought to the highest degree at
Nablous, the ancient Shechem. If one of them in
that town is bribed by the buyer of wheat, not only

does he bring his measure to take up the largest possible quantity, but in raising it up after it is flowing over, he secretly lifts up with the hand supporting the bottom of the measure a considerable quantity of grain, which is so swiftly and adroitly done as to escape the observation of the *fellahh* who is selling it.

I have taken means carefully to ascertain the capacity of the Palestine *timneh*.[1] It is true, different kinds of wheat differ in weight. The following measures give the contents in the case of the best quality. A *timneh* filled up to the brim, without being shaken or pressed, weighs six *rottles* and one-sixth, or just thirty-seven pounds. The same *timneh*, not only filled to the top but running over, that is, piled up above in the shape of a cone, also without being pressed and shaken, weighs seven rottles and one-third, or forty-four pounds. When, however, the measure in question is not only filled till it flows over, but is, at the same time, shaken together and pressed down, it holds just eight rottles, or forty-eight pounds.

No doubt it is to this simple and familiar custom that our Blessed Lord alludes, when He speaks

---

[1] In the villages another measure, about half the size of the *timneh*, is in use, called a *sâah*, which is evidently the same as the סְאָה, *sĕah*, of Scripture (Genesis xviii. 6; I Samuel xxv. 18; 2 Kings vii. 1). The modern *sâah* varies slightly in size in different villages.

under an allegory of the recompense of those liberal
souls who shall assuredly themselves be made
fat. "Give, and it shall be given unto you; good
measure, pressed down, shaken together, running
over, shall they give into your bosom [that is,
into the capacious natural pocket formed by that
part of the loose Eastern shirt which is above
the girdle]. For with what measure ye mete
it shall be measured to you again." [1] The above
facts lend far more power and definiteness to our
Saviour's graphic illustration than we should at first
sight have supposed it to contain. There is no less
than eleven pounds' difference in weight between a
"measure" filled to the brim as we should fill it
here, and one such as I have described filled according to the bountiful method of Bible lands, when
it is "pressed down, shaken together, running over."
In this latter case no less than about 30 per cent.
is added to its worth! Thus largely shall they be
rewarded who have learned to imitate the example of
their God and Saviour in the divine art of generous
giving!

A practice to be constantly noticed throughout
Syria is that of hiding any blood, which may happen
to be spilled on the ground, by covering it over with
the surrounding soil or dust. If while you are on

---

[1] Luke vi. 38. See also Matthew vii. 2, and Mark iv. 24.

a journey a *Bedaween* of your escort only so much as cuts his hand, or suffers from bleeding at the nose, he is very careful to let the blood fall upon the earth, without leaving any stain upon his clothing or person, and he then and there buries it out of sight by scraping over it the sand or dust of the desert before he proceeds on his way. The reason which they give for this observance I have not been able to discover. Most probably it comes from the thought in Numbers that blood pollutes the land if left to lie upon it,[1] and from the plain direction in the case of the huntsman who caught any beast or fowl, to " pour out the blood thereof, and cover it with dust." [2] It is reasonable to suppose that this direction, like many other matters contained in the law, embodied and sanctioned an already well-known and universal practice. Very likely it arose from anxiety lest any blood appearing upon the ground might by any possibility be construed to represent some act of violence, and thus, in the language of Scripture, " cause fury to come up to take vengeance." This, in a land where the law of blood-revenge causing endless sanguinary family feuds is so stringent, may well be no imaginary fear. In any case, it is deeply interesting to mark its observance at the present day. It would seem to be referred to in the strong figurative language of

---

[1] Numbers xxxv. 33.   [2] Leviticus xvii. 13.

several passages, notably that where Job in the
bitterness of his soul cries,

"Earth, cover not thou my blood."[1]

A very striking Scripture in connection with this
Eastern usage is that in Ezekiel, where God foretells
the judgments coming upon Jerusalem at the hands
of the Chaldeans. These judgments are declared
to be a retribution for the reckless violence and
cruelty that had openly stalked through her streets.
" For her blood is in the midst of her; she set it
upon the bare rock; she hath not *poured it upon the
ground, to cover it with dust*. That it may cause
fury to come up to take vengeance, I have set her
blood upon the bare rock, that it should not be
covered."[2] There is here a force of meaning that
might at first sight be overlooked. Jerusalem, as I
shall have occasion elsewhere to explain at length,
is essentially a rock city. The rock crops up to
the surface in every part of it. In ancient times,
before the rugged slopes and precipices of limestone
and indurated chalk were choked up and covered
over, as they are now, by mountains of débris, it
appeared, as at the fortress of Jebus, with its walls
resting on rock scarps in some places fifty feet high.
Hence one of its proud titles was " the Tableland
rock," a name given to it in another passage where

[1] Job xvi. 18.   [2] Ezekiel xxiv. 7, 8.

its judgment is denounced.[1]   But this natural stronghold of Zion, alas! was constantly the scene of internal robbery and oppression, of bigotry, cruelty, and persecution.   This history of violence was summed up by our Blessed Lord in the solemn words, " It cannot be that a prophet perish out of Jerusalem," [2] that is, in any other place but that guilty city!   Thus in the passage I have cited from Ezekiel, God says, as it were, " I have not allowed these cruel persecutions to take place in the provinces, but in Jerusalem, of which you boast as ' the tableland rock,' that there on this stony stronghold you might not be able to find soil enough to cover up and hide from my sight the blood of the martyred saints and the innocent poor who have suffered at your hands, but that it might remain exposed, as a witness against you, and ' cause fury to come up,' by crying to me for vengeance!"

The lighting of camp-fires is a constant and very noticeable feature of journeys in the Holy Land. Fuel for this purpose is afforded by the low, woody, herbaceous growth, partaking largely of a thorny nature, which abounds in the deserts, and is to be met with by the wayside in most parts of the

---

[1] Jeremiah xxi. 13.   [2] Luke xiii. 33.

country. The "fire of thorns" is often alluded to
in the Old Testament, and every resident in Palestine has reason to know what a familiar sight it is.[1]
Easterns, who have a great dread of darkness and a
passionate fondness for light, seem to rejoice to seize
every opportunity of making these bonfires, and continuing them far into the night. They particularly
delight in the crackling and the bright flames which
thorn bushes specially throw out. They kindle
these fires, however, as much for protection as for
pleasure. The lurid light thus given serves to
scare away the wild beasts which come out at night
in many lonely places, and also to show to those
on the watch the approach of thieves and robbers.
When travelling under the escort of *Bedaween* Arabs
in certain dangerous parts of the desert, travellers
have observed that their wild escort keep up watch-
fires round the camp all night, while the "keepers,"
or guards, shout out at intervals to render the protection more complete. On one occasion, while
travelling through the waterless desert leading to
Palmyra, when within a short distance of its ruins,

[1] Psalm cxviii. 12 ; Isaiah xxxiii. 12. Sometimes the mention
of fire in connection with thorns refers to large conflagrations
kindled in autumn. These extensive fires are lighted to clear
the stubble lands of their wild growth, amongst which thorny
plants of many kinds are very numerous (Exodus xxii. 6 ; 2 Samuel
xxiii. 6, 7 ; Nahum i. 10). The context generally shows which kind
of fire is meant.

I had to pass a large camp of the '*Anazeh* tribe of
Bedaween.   I was travelling all night, accompanied
by a friend and a government escort of soldiers.
For an hour before we drew near to them, we saw
large bright fires encircling the encampment, and
we had to ride far out of our way in order to avoid
them.   The flames of these fires were kept up till
daybreak.

There would seem to be a plain allusion to this
practice in the promise of Jehovah's safeguard over
Jerusalem in millennial times.   " Jerusalem shall
abide as the country parts, for the multitude of men
and cattle therein.   And I, saith Jehovah, will
be unto her a wall of fire round about." [1]   All
Eastern cities to this day are surrounded with high
massive walls and stout iron-plated and iron-barred
gates.   The security, wealth, and safety of Israel's
metropolis during the fulness of Messiah's kingdom
is shown in this representation by its walls being
thrown down, its boundaries immensely enlarged,
and its being inhabited like a vast camp over which
the Lord Himself continually watches.

Still clearer is the reference to these camp-fires
kindled for protection, in a passage in Isaiah.   The
prophet, after administering comfort to the faithful
in Israel, proceeds to warn the faithless and self-
righteous of the utter futility of their carnal efforts

[1] Zechariah ii. 4, 5.

to seek salvation. To all who fear Jehovah he
says—

> " Let him that walketh in darkness,
>   and hath no light,
>   Trust in the name of Jehovah,
>   And stay himself upon his God." [1]

But to the unbelievers he cries, in the next verse,

> " Behold, all ye that kindle a fire,
>   That gird you about with flames !
>   Walk in the light of your fire,
>   And in the flames ye have lighted ;
>   This shall ye have from my hand ;
>   Ye shall lie down in sorrow."

Here the girding about with flames, evidently as a
means of protection in the darkness, is connected
with laying down to sleep. Yet their rest shall
be broken by trouble and sorrow, notwithstanding
all the flames of the watch-fires with which they
are surrounded.

Speaking of the great services that the Jews
are to receive from those Gentile nations which
have persecuted them in the past at the time when
they are to be restored to their own land, the Lord
declares by the prophet Isaiah—

> " I will lift up my hand to the nations,
>
>   .   .   .   .   .   .
>
>   And thy daughters shall be carried upon
>   their shoulders." [2]

---

[1] Isaiah l. 10.   [2] Isaiah xlix. 22.

Here is a most significant picture, and yet one the meaning and power of which is entirely hidden from the Western reader.

Children in the East, though sometimes folded to the bosom, by being placed within the wide natural pocket of the robe, or slung in a scarf across the back, or borne astride upon the hip, are not carried upon the arm in that laborious fashion common with us. Instead of this, as soon as the swaddling-clothes are removed—those long cotton bandages which, during its earliest infancy, bind the body of the helpless child into a small mummy-like bundle [1]—the nurse begins to accustom her charge to sit astride upon her shoulder. She teaches it at first to support itself by clinging with its baby fingers to the top of her head, while she herself simply places one hand against the lower part of the child's back. This method is generally adopted when mothers or nurses carry their children, and Egyptian sculptures show that it was just the same four thousand years ago. It serves two important ends. First of all, it lightens labour, helps to

---

[1] Luke ii. 7, 12. See also Ezekiel xvi. 4; and observe the very bold figure in Job xxxviii. 9. It will explain the allusion in Ezekiel xvi. 4, "Thou wast not salted at all, nor swaddled at all," to bear in mind, that, to this day in Palestine, salt is rubbed into the body of a new-born infant, before it is wrapped round with swaddling clothes, that is, plain bands of calico some six inches wide by three yards in length.

improve rather than to injure the figure of the
nurse by expanding instead of contracting her
chest, strengthening her spine, and making her more
upright, and, when the child has learned, as it soon
does, to support itself alone, possesses the great
advantage of leaving both her arms and hands free.
But more than this, it teaches every child from its
earliest years to ride on horseback. It exercises
from infancy those muscles of the knees by which
the proper riding grip should be taken, giving in
after years that fearless and immovable seat for
which Eastern equestrians are justly famous, and
which it is so necessary to possess in a country
where all journeys have to be performed in the
saddle, and where women sit astride a horse like
men. An Emeer, or prince of the Lebanon, will
place a sovereign between his knee and the saddle,
and after a day's coursing or hawking will produce
it again. I mention this in passing, but it will be
seen at once that "to be carried on the shoulder"
means to receive the tender and respectful care
which the nurse or slave-girl of Palestine invariably shows to her young charge. This graphic
and picturesque figure tells how Israel will find
in their former proud persecutors humble and
loyal servants. The new-born children of God
will be carried home by the awe-stricken and
penitent nations as by eager and willing slaves!

This meaning is confirmed by the following verses :—

> "And kings shall be thy nursing fathers,
> And their princesses thy nursing mothers.
> They shall bow down to thee with their
>   face toward the earth,
> And shall lick up the dust of thy feet." [1]

It must be also carefully observed that girls throughout the East do not at all receive the same attention as boys. Neither parents nor nurses treat them with anything like the consideration that they show towards " a man-child." While they delight to lift up the latter to ride upon their shoulders, the girls are left for the most part to run about by themselves. In a word, the order which Christianity has introduced amongst us is entirely reversed. It is the natural result of that inferior estimate of woman, which is the outcome of the polygamy that has prevailed in these lands from time immemorial. There is, therefore, a touch of intense meaning given to the picture of the honour which God has in store for His ancient people, when He declares,

> " Thy *daughters* shall be carried upon their shoulders."

Amongst countless examples of metaphor—for this is the figure most frequently used in Scripture—occurs the highly poetical language of David—

[1] Isaiah xlix. 23.

> " If I take the wings of the morning,
> And dwell in the uttermost parts of the sea,
> Even there shall thy hand lead me,
> And thy right hand shall hold me." [1]

The bold metaphorical use of the leading by the right hand will be dealt with by itself in another place. But the former figure, " wings of the morning," to a Western is not a little obscure. For my part, I cannot doubt that we are to understand certain beautiful light clouds as thus poetically described. I have observed invariably that in the late spring-time, in summer, and yet more especially in the autumn, white clouds are to be seen in Palestine. They only occur at the earliest hours of morning, just previous to and at the time of sunrise. It is the total absence of clouds at all other parts of the day, except during the short period of the winter rains, that lends such striking solemnity and force to those descriptions of the Second Advent where our Lord is represented as coming in the clouds. [2] This feature of His majesty loses all its meaning in lands like ours, in which clouds are of such common occurrence that they are

---

[1] Psalm cxxxix. 9, 10.

[2] Daniel vii. 13 ; Matthew xxiv. 30 ; xxvi. 64 ; Mark xiii. 26 ; xiv. 62 ; Luke xxi. 27 ; Revelations i. 7 ; xiv. 14. Hence, too, the very special significance attaching to a cloud sheltering Israel during the hot and absolutely cloudless months of summer in their desert wanderings through the burning valleys of Sinai (Exodus xiii. 21 ; Numbers x. 34 ; Psalm cv. 39)—to a cloud descending

rarely absent from the sky.   The morning clouds of
summer and autumn are always of a brilliant silvery
white, save at such times as they are dyed with the
delicate opal tints of dawn.   They hang low upon
the mountains of Judah, and produce effects of
indescribable beauty, as they float far down in the
valleys, or rise to wrap themselves around the
summit of the hills.   In almost every instance, by
about seven o'clock the heat has dissipated these
fleecy clouds, and to the vivid Eastern imagination
morn has folded her outstretched wings.

Hosea alludes especially to this fugitive phenomenon of the hot season, when he cries of Israel,

"Your goodness is like the morning cloud." [1]

Moreover, clouds are intimately connected in Palestine with "the sea," that is the Mediterranean, "the
Great Sea westward."   When Elijah was earnestly
pleading with God for rain, He sent His servant
up to the heights of Carmel to gather the first
intimation of an answer to his prayer.   " Go up,
I pray," he said, " and look towards the sea."   At

on Sinai, some time in June (Exodus xix. 16; xxiv. 15)—to a cloud
overshadowing the Mount of Transfiguration, apparently in summer
(Matthew xvii. 5)—to a cloud receiving the ascending Saviour towards the end of May or the beginning of June (Acts i. 9)—and
to clouds mentioned in other passages.

[1] Hosea vi. 4. In our version it is "as *a* morning cloud," but
the above rendering, which is the true translation of the Hebrew,
brings out the special allusion very distinctly.

his seventh ascent he was able to report, " Behold, there ariseth a little cloud out of the sea." [1] This is still the direction from which all the clouds in Palestine invariably come. The Arabs call the west wind "the father of rain," in allusion to its bringing up the clouds from their home on "the Great Sea westward." The "morning cloud," or mass of dense white mist, consists of the moisture brought up from the Mediterranean by the prevalent westerly winds of summer and autumn, which becomes condensed on passing over the colder night air of the land. I shall have occasion to speak at length of the formation and inestimable value of these remarkable clouds when describing the "dew," for they constitute a most peculiar and important feature of the climate of Palestine. A consideration, however, of the foregoing facts will at once display the appropriateness of the bold and beautiful metaphor—

> " If I take the wings of the morning,
>   And dwell in the uttermost parts of the sea."

Next to their remarkably fine erect figures, perhaps nothing strikes one more in the appearance of the lightly-clad peasant women of Palestine than their long, pendant breasts. This feature may, I think, be partly accounted for by the great length

[1] 1 Kings xviii. 42–45.

of time during which they suckle their children. Infants are seldom, if ever, weaned amongst the *fellahheen*, or villagers, under two years of age. It is, however, no extraordinary thing for a mother to continue to give a "man-child" the breast till the end of his fourth or fifth year. Indeed, our Bethlehem nurse assured us that she had known the case of a favourite child whose mother had not weaned it until it was seven years of age! Girls would never be treated in this way, meeting as they do on all occasions with marked neglect. The native women believe that the longer a child is allowed to remain at the breast the stronger he grows. When, therefore, a boy appears one of great promise, or is a first-born, or seems likely to be the only child, the mother, if it is possible, nurses him until he is four years of age.

These facts are really important as rendering intelligible the early history of little Samuel. Her child was granted to Hannah at a time when she was hopelessly barren, in answer to special prayer, and she had dedicated him before his birth to the Lord by a solemn vow, in which she declared she would "give him unto Jehovah all the days of his life." When he was born Hannah determined that it would be lawful for her to keep him until he was weaned, and doubtless, like all the women of Palestine at the present day, believed that the longer she could nurse him the stronger and better he would become. She, therefore, proposed to stay at home, and not accompany her husband on his yearly pilgrimage to Shiloh until the child was taken from the breast, and "then," she said, "I will bring him, that he may appear before Jehovah, and abide there for ever." This decision thoroughly approved itself to her affectionate husband. Elkanah said to her: "Do what seemeth thee good; tarry until thou have weaned him; only Jehovah establish His word. So the woman abode, and gave her son suck until she weaned him."[1] How many yearly festivals passed by before that event we are not told; but, from what has been said above, we cannot doubt that according to every usage and feeling of the East at the present day, little Samuel was not weaned until he was from three to five years of age, and therefore quite old enough to be left by himself with the aged high priest, and to enter at once upon some childish service in the sanctuary. Doubtless when the infant Moses was so providentially restored to his mother. she kept him at the breast much as Hannah kept Samuel, if only that she might have her child under her own care as long as possible.

Everything, too, in the account in Genesis of the circumstances of Isaac's weaning would seem to

[1] 1 Samuel i. 21–23.

point to this remarkable child of promise as also having been nursed by his mother for several years.[1] I have noticed with intense interest when reading that admirable work, *The Approaching End of the Age*, that the author calls attention to the fact that the four hundred years of affliction and bondage foretold as coming upon Abraham's seed starts *from the time when Isaac was five years old*. He adds: " To this day it is a matter of conjecture what the event was which marked that year, though there is little doubt that it was the casting out of the bond-woman and her son on the occasion of the mocking of the heir of promise by the natural seed. This mocking, or ' persecuting' (Gal. iv. 29), is the first affliction of Abraham's seed of which we have any record, and its result demonstrated that it was in Isaac the seed was to be called."[2] These statements are no doubt correct, but they contain what at first sight appears to the Western reader a grave difficulty. The mocking of the promised seed took place at the feast when Isaac was weaned. That he should have been five years old on the day that he was weaned seems unaccountable to us, but constitutes no difficulty whatever in Palestine. It is in perfect keeping with the practice of the

---

[1] Genesis xxi. 8–10.
[2] *The Approaching End of the Age*, by Mr. H. Grattan Guinness, 2nd edition, p. 478.

D

East at the present day. Under the circumstances of his being a remarkable, long waited for, and only child, it is rather to have been expected than otherwise, that Sarah's son should have reached his fourth or fifth year before he was entirely taken from the breast.

A similar explanation is necessary if we are to attach any distinct or literal meaning to the words of Isaiah—

> "Whom doth he teach knowledge?
> And whom doth he make to understand instruction?
> Those weaned from the milk,
> Those withdrawn from the breasts." [1]

Children as soon as they are weaned amongst us could not " understand instruction," but in Palestine weaning takes place at an age when they can begin to be taught knowledge. Almost all Eastern boys can both speak and understand what is spoken to them when first " withdrawn from the breasts." It is indeed a tender age at which to begin, but one that no wise parent will allow to pass by unimproved.

Again, our Blessed Lord's quotation,

> " Out of the mouth of babes and sucklings thou
> hast perfected praise," [2]

viewed thus, becomes capable of a literal sense.

If we consider a comparison used by the Psalmist

---

[1] Isaiah xxviii. 9.
[2] Matthew xxi. 16, quoted from Psalm viii. 2, Septuagint version.

in this light, we shall see in it a new power and
beauty.   The words to which I allude, attributed
in the heading of the Psalm to David, are those in
which he declares—

> " I have calmed and quieted my soul,
>   Like a child that is weaned by his mother,
>   My soul within me is even as a weaned child." [1]

The man after God's own heart is speaking of his
conscious humility.   He has but just before declared
that his heart is not haughty, neither has he exercised himself in great matters.   In contrast to such
proud bearing, his spirit, he tells us, is meek and
gentle, like that of a young child of three years of
age.   To us the idea of a weaned child conveys only
the thought of helpless and unintelligent infancy,
and would, therefore, have no force in this connection.   But, viewed in the above light, David's words
are not only full of significant meaning, but are no
less than an expression of the same truth taught
afterwards by David's Lord, when He "called to
Him a little child, and set him in the midst of
them, and said, ' Verily I say unto you, Except
ye turn, and become as little children, ye shall
in no wise enter into the kingdom of heaven.
Whosoever therefore shall humble himself as this
little child, the same is the greatest in the kingdom
of heaven.' " [2]

---

[1] Psalm cxxxi. 2.   [2] Matthew xviii. 2-4.

Throughout Palestine, gardens, orchards, and vineyards, unlike other cultivated spots, are always enclosed, and the fence employed in almost every instance is the common enclosure wall of the country, called a *jĕdar*. This rude and primitive construction is formed of rough, shapeless, unhewn stones, of all sizes. Long practice has made the people very skilful in making the *jĕdars*, and the hard marble-like *mizzey* rock, which crops up to the surface in every part of the country, affords them abundant and excellent material for this purpose. The ground is first smoothed, and the stones are then piled up, about three feet in width at the bottom, and gradually narrowing towards the top. No mortar of any kind is employed, the stones merely being laid so as to fit closely together. The height varies in ordinary cases from four to six feet. Sometimes they are carried up as high as twelve feet. The whole construction is of course comparatively fragile; but in some ways this is an advantage, for a thief, whether man or beast, cannot easily climb over it without displacing and throwing down the loose stones, and so giving notice of his approach. Indeed it is dangerous to attempt to surmount it in the dark, for the climber runs a great risk of being thrown down and crushed by the fall of some huge fragment of its rocky contents. These walls are sometimes armed with dried thorn bushes placed upon the top.

The heavy rain-storms of winter constantly bring down portions of the *jĕdars*, by undermining the soft foundation of earth upon which they are laid, but they are readily repaired at a slight expense, without the use of any fresh materials.

Now it is deeply interesting to notice that these very walls are frequently mentioned in the Old Testament. The Hebrew word *gadair*,[1] which is twice written *geder*,[2] and has a feminine form, *gedairah*,[3] is evidently the equivalent of the Arabic *jĕdar*. The softening of the hard *g* into *j* in the Arabic transliteration of all Hebrew words is a well-recognised fact. In this way the Hebrew *gamal*, a camel, becomes *jemel* in Arabic, and the town of Gannim, or En-Gannim, on the south of the plain of Esdraelon, is now *Jenin*. The feminine form *gedairah* is generally used of "folds" for sheep, and is the expression employed by the two and a half tribes when, seeking their inheritance in Moab, Gilead, and Bashan, they said, "We will build sheep *folds* here for our cattle."[4] The common sheepfolds of Palestine are to this day large enclosures formed of the *jĕdars* which I have described, and hence the name *gedairah*, or, as in modern Arabic, *jĕdarah*. When Israel's final restoration in millennial times

---

[1] גָּדֵר.   [2] גֶּדֶר.   [3] גְּדֵרָה.

[4] Numbers xxxii. 16. The same word is translated "folds" in verses 24, 36. See also 1 Samuel xxiv. 3, and Zephaniah ii. 6.

is pictured under the gathering together of a strayed flock, the prophet cries—

" A day [cometh] for building thy *jĕdars*." [1]

When the angel of the Lord went out to withstand Balaam, " he stood in a path of the vineyards, a *jĕdar* being on this side and a *jĕdar* on that." [2] Nothing could be more natural than this description. Vividly it recalls to my mind places where I have had to pass through similar narrow passages, only a few feet across, separating the massive vineyard hedges of such rough unhewn stone. These loose unmortared walls afford endless hot dusty crevices in which the serpent tribe delight. They can, moreover, be easily and swiftly thrown down by any mischievously-disposed person. There is, therefore, far more force, than appears in our version, in that proverb which tells how deeds of violence and wrong recoil on the doer—" Whoso breaketh down a *jĕdar*, a serpent biteth him." [3]

The Psalmist, comparing Israel to a vineyard of the Lord's planting, cries of its ruinous state in his day—

" Why hast thou broken down its *jĕdars*,
So that all who pass by the way do pluck it ?
The boar out of the tangled thicket doth waste it." [4]

---

[1] Micah vii. 11.   [2] Numbers xxii. 24.   [3] Ecclesiastes x. 8.
[4] Psalm lxxx. 12.

In autumn the wild boars, who are very fond of grapes, still come up by night around the Hebron vineyards, to plunder and waste them if they can only find a breach in the *jĕdars*. The peasants at this season lie in wait outside these stone enclosures after dark in order to shoot them.

A *jĕdar* naturally came to be used as a figure of general defence and protection. Hence Ezra, in his humble prayer of confession, recounting the mercies of God, says: He " hath extended mercy to us, . . . to give us a *jĕdar* in Judah." [1]

To " make up or repair the *jĕdar*," that familiar operation to be witnessed each winter in Palestine, when the pieces of stone which have fallen down are piled up again, came in the same way to mean metaphorically the setting right of that which was wrong amongst the people of God, and so restoring the Divine protection.[2] When the foundation has given way, and a wall of this kind once begins to crumble and topple down, nothing could better image a condition of helpless weakness. In a passage, which requires a different rendering from that given in our version, David so employs it. He has just been rejoicing in the strength of God, his Rock, abiding in whom he knows that he will remain unmoved. At the same time he confesses his own utter weakness and helplessness under

<hr/>

[1] Ezra ix. 9.   [2] Ezekiel xiii. 5, xxii. 30.

the onslaught of his fierce foes, with whom he
thus remonstrates :

> " How long will ye rush upon a man,
> Will ye break him down, all of you,
> As a bowing wall, or a tottering *jĕdar ?* " [1]

At noon, in Syria, the heat during summer is very
great, and though it is tempered by the rare dry-
ness of a climate naturally most healthy, all who
can possibly do so desist at that hour from work,
and seek a place of shelter and rest.   Even labouring
people endeavour at this time to get away from the
sun, and to spend an hour in sleep, while in the
towns and villages the busy hum of life almost
entirely ceases.   Jeremiah, who draws such dark
pictures of lamentation and woe, on several occasions
heightens the terrors of threatened judgments by
describing them as coming at noon, an hour when
both besieger and besieged would, under all ordinary
circumstances, alike take rest.   Speaking of the
Chaldean descent on Jerusalem, he says—

> " Prepare ye war against her.
> Arise, and let us go up at *noon !* " [2]

And again he declares of guilty Zion—

> " I bring upon them, against the mother of the strong
> young man,

---

[1] Psalm lxii. 3.　　　　[2] Jeremiah vi. 4.

A spoiler at *noon-day!*
I cause to fall upon her suddenly anguish and terrors." [1]

The shepherd in the arid and glaring deserts is especially exposed to the heat, and at twelve o'clock on a summer-day, when the rays of the sun strike almost perpendicularly down, is sorely tried to find shelter for his flock. Yet the good shepherd, I have observed, constantly manages to do so. There are in most of the wilderness pastures of the Holy Land high cliffs or ledges of rock, which almost overhang their base, and are arranged at such an angle to the zenith that even when the sun is at its height they still afford a thin but precious strip of shade. Here the shepherd resorts with his sheep, and you may often see the flock extending in a long line so as to avail themselves of the narrow shelter. Even when this is not sufficient in length to afford standing room for all, the sheep may be seen stretching beyond, and taking refuge, as it were, one behind another. Indeed this finding a sheltered resting-place for his charge at the midday hour forms a part of the daily routine of the shepherd's life.

There is a beautiful allusion to this, and one which has, I think, been hitherto overlooked, in the pastoral imagery of the Song of Songs. The bride, seeking the king, cries—

[1] Jeremiah xv. 8. See also xx. 16.

"Tell me, thou whom my soul loveth,
Where thou shepherdest [thy flock],
Where thou *restest* [*them*] *at noon?*"[1]

The soul has its seasons of labour and rest, but in
both, if it is to be at peace, it must be with Christ.
In the burning noontide of life, when scorched by
temptation and sin, or amidst the fiery heat of
persecution, we may be sure of finding safety and
refreshment in Jesus, if we flee unto Him to hide
us. Our Good Shepherd is in Himself such a place
of refuge, "the shadow of a great rock in a weary
land," that is, "a land of exhausting heat."[2]

Aqueducts are, and always must have been, very
common and familiar objects in the Holy Land.
They still are, too, and must ever have been, of
vital importance in a country where good springs
are in many parts comparatively few. Two things,
therefore, are highly improbable. First, that the
inspired writers, who drew their simple but striking
figures especially from horticultural subjects, should
have failed in a single instance to allude to these
precious water channels. Secondly, that the exceedingly primitive, rich, and precise Hebrew tongue
should lack a special technical term by which to
describe them. For my own part, since my residence in Palestine led me to realise the prominent

[1] Song of Solomon i. 7.   [2] Isaiah xxxii. 2.

place that aqueducts have always occupied in that land, I have felt that they must have been spoken of by name in the Bible.

This mention appeared to me plain when afterwards seeking a meaning for the word ăpheek,[1] which occurs eighteen times in the Old Testament, besides forming the names of towns such as Aphaik, near Bethhoron, and Aphaikah, near Hebron.[2] That our translators could make but little of this term is evident. They have rendered it by no less than seven different words, and the one they have adopted most frequently, "river," cannot possibly be its true meaning! The word is derived from aphak,[3] which, in all the places where it occurs in the Old Testament, bears the sense of "restraining" or "forcing."[4] Now the leading idea of an aqueduct is that which forces or constrains a stream of water to flow in a given direction. The strength of one of the high pressure aqueducts, that formerly brought the water of a distant spring to the Holy City, in a direct line up and down the slopes of the mountains, was very great. Each pipe consisted of a large

[1] אֲפִיק

[2] I Samuel iv. 1 ; Joshua xv. 53. Spelt in our version Aphek and Aphekah.

[3] אָפַק

[4] "Joseph could not *restrain himself*" (Genesis xlv. 1) ; "*I forced myself*" (1 Samuel xiii. 12) ; "Haman *restrained* himself " (Esther v. 10), &c.

block of stone bored through the centre. Several
of these were recently discovered in position. The
aqueducts were generally made of earthenware pipes,
laid in thick beds of a cement largely formed of
hhomrah, or crushed pottery, which in the course
of time became as hard as stone. Sometimes they
were cut as grooves in the limestone of the hillsides. At others, but more rarely, they were narrow
open ditches, by which the waters of a river were
carried to another part of the plain. In one or
two instances they consisted of a deep underground
channel, connecting a number of little pools, or pits,
such as those now in ruins at *Ain Fusail*, and the
Vale of Siddim in the Jordan valley. In each case
the chief idea of the aqueduct was the constraint
put upon the water of spring, stream, or pool, by
which it was forced to run in a prepared channel.
The word *ăpheek*, besides its strict technical meaning, appears to have had other senses. It would
seem to have signified the natural subterranean
channels which supply springs, and also to have
been the special name for the narrow, rocky, aqueduct-like beds of some mountain streams.

If we take a few of the passages where it
occurs, the appropriateness and beauty of the rendering I now suggest will at once appear. A
striking instance of the use of this word is
found in the highly poetic description of the

strength of the hippopotamus given by Jehovah
Himself—

"His bones are aqueducts of brass." [1]

The figure rendered thus becomes one of magnificent boldness, whereas the translation in our
version, "*strong pieces* of brass," is without any
warrant, and possesses no special significance. The
word occurs again in describing the rugged ridges of
thick tubular skin, seventeen in number, which, like
shields, protect the invulnerable crocodile. [2]

This explanation adds new meaning and beauty
to the opening words of the 42d Psalm. These are
literally—

"As the hind panteth over the aqueducts,
So panteth my soul after thee, O God." [3]

In our Bible it reads "panteth after the water
brooks." But the picture of the Psalmist is far

---

[1] Job xl. 18. [2] Job xli. 15.

[3] Psalm xlii. 1. The Hebrew of the first line of this verse reads:
כְּאַיָּל תַּעֲרֹג עַל אֲפִיקֵי־מָיִם, *kĕayyal ta'ăroag 'al ăpheekaiy-mayim.*
'Al is in almost every instance to be rendered "upon," "over," or
"above," and this makes it impossible to translate *ăpheekaiy-mayim*,
"water brooks," for a deer would not "pant," or "bray," for water
if it were standing over an open stream. The whole force of the
simile is lost in our version, for the thought in the mind of David is
the sense of the inaccessibility of those spiritual privileges which
he had once enjoyed in attending the services of the sanctuary.
The Psalm bears marks of having been written at the season when
he was compelled to fly from Jerusalem by Absalom's rebellion.

stronger than this. He is lamenting his banish-
ment from Zion and all its spiritual privileges in
the manifested presence of Jehovah. He thirsts
after God, and longs to taste again the joy of
His house, like the parched and weary hind who
comes to a covered channel, conveying the living
waters of some far-off spring across the intervening
desert. She scents the precious current in its bed of
adamantine cement, or hears its rippling flow close
beneath her feet, or perchance sees it deep down
through one of the narrow air-holes, and, as she
agonises for the inaccessible draught, she "panteth
over the aqueducts!" Yet again the Psalmist
cries—

> "Turn our captivity, O Jehovah,
> As aqueducts in the Negeb." [1]

This Negeb, or South Country, the region stretching below Hebron, being comparatively dry and
waterless, was doubtless irrigated by a system of
small artificial channels. The words of the Psalmist
imply that it is as easy for God to turn Israel back
from Babylonian bondage to their own land, as for
the horticulturist to direct the waters of the spring
to any part of the land he chooses along the channels
of the aqueducts. These aqueducts are spoken of
in connection with the irrigation of the Nile valley,[2]
and the fertility of the mountain districts of Pales-

---

[1] Psalm cxxvi. 4.   [2] Ezekiel xxxii. 6.

tine, more especially Judah.[1] Speaking of millennial times, the prophet declares—

> "The mountains shall drop down new wine,
> And the hills shall flow with milk,
> And all the aqueducts of Judah shall flow with waters."[2]

If this be, as I believe, the true meaning of *ăpheek*, then those places in Palestine which answer to the sites of Aphaik and Aphaikah, and those, of which there are several, bearing the modern name of *Feek*, will probably appear by the memoirs of the Palestine Survey, or from the Survey itself, to stand in connection with some ancient aqueducts, or rocky aqueduct-like ravines.

When a friend of mine, who is an able and observant expositor of Scripture, was travelling in Egypt, during a visit to Alexandria, he noticed quite casually the following incident, which I will give in his own words :—" An aged beggar, whose appearance and garb attracted attention, was slowly pacing the street. A young man, bent on a practical joke, stepped up cautiously behind him, and either pulled or pushed him. The moment he had done so, with great adroitness he stepped back, stooped down in a squatting posture after the fashion of the

---

[1] Ezekiel xxxi. 12. The meaning of *ăpheek* in Ezekiel vi. 3; xxxiv. 13; xxxv. 8; xxxvi. 4, 6, I take to be "ravine," or narrow, rocky, aqueduct-like bed of mountain torrents. It is possible that the word in Joel iii. 18 should be rendered in the same way.

[2] Joel iii. 18.

Easterns, and, assuming an air of innocence and unconcern, commenced scribbling with his finger on the ground. His manner was, in fact, that of a wholly abstracted person, who paid no attention to anything going on around. He behaved as though he saw not the surprise, nor heard the exclamation of the old man."

Perhaps few of the simple actions of our Lord have given rise to more conjecture than that which occurred in the case of the accusation by the Scribes and Pharisees of the woman taken in the act of adultery.[1] Here, however, the precisely similar conduct of an Eastern gives the right explanation, while thoroughly justifying the gloss which our translators have put on the passage by the words they have added in italics. Our Saviour, indignant at the hardened hypocrisy of the accusers, desired to give them an impressive rebuke by treating them with silent contempt, and, by studied and well-understood manner, affecting to be entirely indifferent to their insincere charge. Jesus, we read, " stooped down, and with his finger wrote on the ground, [*as though he heard them not*]."

---

[1] John viii. 6. I am aware that the best critics reject the whole narrative in which these words appear. But as long as it holds its place in our version, and there is any probability that the circumstance actually occurred, the above explanation ought to be generally known. While this work is going through the press, the Revised Version of the New Testament has appeared, in which the passage is retained, but placed within brackets, and the words in italics are left out.

CHAPTER III.

MISCELLANEOUS ILLUSTRATIONS.

(Continued.)

"Every scribe who has been made a disciple in respect to the kingdom of heaven is like unto a man that is a householder, who bringeth forth out of his treasury things new and old."—MATTHEW xiii. 52.

THE power of lungs possessed by both men and women in the East is very remarkable. In giving an account of sifting, I shall have occasion to describe the way in which the sifter aids the simple but searching process by blowing with much strength across the surface of the sieve instead of using a fan. It is not, however, the only trying use to which the people of Palestine, who seem to utterly despise all labour-saving apparatus, are in the habit of putting their singularly strong chests. On all ordinary occasions, when making or reviving a fire, they employ their mouths, where we should employ a pair of bellows. Placing their lips close to the wood or charcoal, with great and continuously sus-

E

tained force they blow upon the embers until they give out a warm and steady blaze. I have repeatedly watched my servants kindling a flame in this laborious manner. The practice is universal, and indeed they call this blowing " making the fire." There are, I believe, pointed references to it in the Bible. Speaking of the judgments to come upon Jerusalem, God says, " I will blow against thee the fire of my wrath, ... Thou shalt be for fuel to the fire." [1] Of the hypocrite's end it is said by Zophar the Naamathite—

"A fire not blown shall consume him," [2]

that is, " a supernatural fire ;" for this was probably a cruel allusion to " the fire of God," the lightning that fell from heaven, and destroyed Job's flocks and shepherds. [3]

One of the great inconveniences of life in the tents of the *Bedaween* Arabs, and in the houses of the *fellahheen*, which are built without chimneys, is the kindling of wood fires in the midst of an apartment, from whence the smoke, having no regular place of egress, spreads into every corner. In the houses of the rich braziers of charcoal are employed, and as their contents are carefully burnt in the open air to a white heat before they are brought into the midst

---

[1] Ezekiel xxi. 31, 32.   [2] Job xx. 26.   [3] Job i. 16.

of a room, they give out no fumes of any kind, while diffusing a genial warmth. It was on such a " fire of coals," that is, small pieces of charcoal—the only coal known in Bible lands—that the angel of the Lord baked a cake for Elijah, and that Christ, when appearing to His disciples at the Sea of Galilee, prepared fish and bread.[1] It was around such a brazier of charcoal that Peter sat with the servants and the officers in the High Priest's palace when he denied the Lord.[2] But in the homes of the people at large, and even in the tents of Arab sheikhs and the houses of some head-men in the poorer villages, wood fires are, for several purposes, the only ones employed.

I was entertained for three days in the spring of 1872 by the Arab sheikh who presides in the village of *Tudmoor*, the ancient Tadmor in the wilderness built by Solomon,[3] which is now contained, with much ground besides to spare, within the still-standing curtain walls of the vast temple of the sun. His home presented one of those wonderful contrasts of ancient grandeur and still more ancient simplicity which lend the height of picturesqueness to modern Syria. The guest chamber on this occasion was

---

[1] 1 Kings xix. 5, 6 ; John xxi. 9.   [2] John xviii. 18.

[3] 2 Chronicles viii. 4. This remote spot, the Ultima Thule of Syrian travel, is better known by its later Greek name of Palmyra, which, like its Hebrew name, Tadmor, is indicative of an oasis of palm-trees, some of which remain to the present day.

unfortunately full, and I and my companion had to share it with some eight native friends who were also visiting the sheikh at this time. The room was far from large, and, as it had to serve as usual for our bedroom by night as well as our dining and sitting-room by day, we suffered considerable inconvenience. But next to the plague of vermin, introduced by the Arab guests, nothing tried me more than the smoke, which rose from the large wood fire, kindled from time to time on the stone floor in the midst of the room. Before daybreak the servant came in, and stepping over the bodies of the sleeping guests as we lay on our simple mattresses on the floor, lighted a pile of wood, much of which was in a green condition, and proceeded to prepare our morning cups of coffee. However difficult it had been to sleep amid the attacks of countless small tormentors during the night, this was even worse, and I now found myself forced to get up. The wreaths of smoke got into my throat and made me cough, while also causing the most painful irritation to my eyes and nostrils. Our host proceeded to invite us as usual to gather round the fire and drink coffee with him. This was the most trying part of the day. At such time there was no escaping from the fumes, and my eyes were constantly filled with water, and became painfully inflamed. Had not the stringent rules of Eastern etiquette, rendering it imperatively necessary that I should drink my host's coffee, and the cold of the grey dawn without equally constrained me, I should have fled from the house to escape the torturing smoke.

In some large dwellings chimney-places exist of a rude kind, with a hearth enclosed by slabs of stone, sometimes with an andiron. But the houses generally are built without chimneys, and the fire is lighted in the centre of the room, and the smoke allowed to escape where it can. Doubtless it was this primitive and universal practice which gave rise to the expressive proverb—

"As smoke to the eyes,
So is the sluggard to them that send him."[1]

The irritation and annoyance caused by an idle and worthless servant is thus forcefully and graphically described under a most familiar figure. Fortunately these fires, save in the coldest weather, are not continually burning, but are only lighted at such time as guests drop in and coffee has to be prepared. In the severest parts of winter, however, when the family can afford the fuel, they are kept up all day. The constant smoke arising from green wood must in such cases prove a most painful nuisance to those who have to stay in the house. It would seem that this is the allusion of the Most High when, of

[1] Proverbs x. 26.

His rebellious, idolatrous, self-righteous people, He declares—

> "These are a smoke in my nose,
> A fire that burneth all the day."[1]

David, when exiled in the barren wilderness of Judea, amid terrible sufferings and privation, and almost in despair at the long loss of spiritual privileges, cries—

> "My tears have been my food day and night."[2]

To an English ear such a figure of speech sounds strained and unnatural. Tears, it would seem to us, might indeed have been called by David his drink, but that they should be said to be his "food," or meat, appears at first sight very inappropriate.

Yet in the East nothing could be more proper than this bold but perfectly consistent representation. Solid meat is, and always must have been, comparatively rare in Syria. Beef is seldom or never eaten, mutton in summer is very scarce, and lean goat's-flesh is in many parts all that can be

---

[1] Isaiah lxv. 5.

[2] Psalm xlii. 3. The word "food" here, לֶחֶם, *lehhem*, in most instances translated "bread" in our version, is edible provision of any kind. It is used of manna (Exodus xvi. 4, 8, 12), of mallows (Job xxx. 4), of fruit (Jeremiah xi. 19), of the whole of the rich provision at Joseph's feast (Genesis xliii. 25, 31), and of the flesh of animal sacrifices (Numbers xxviii. 2). It frequently occurs in the technical sense of "bread" made of wheat, barley, millet, or some other grain.

obtained for several months in the year. The impossibility, owing to the warmth of the weather, of
hanging the meat, even when it can be procured,
renders it tough, and makes it necessary for culinary
purposes to broil or stew it to excess. The invariable method of preparing animal food throughout
the East is that indicated in the injunction to Peter
in the heavenly vision, namely, "kill and eat."[1]
When thus cooked immediately after it is slaugh-
tered, and while the carcass is still warm, the meat
is far more tender and good than when it has been
hung for a day, but not quite so tender or well
flavoured as when eaten in that state of incipient
corruption in which we partake of it in the West.
All the *Bedaween* Arab sheikhs, who very rarely
take meat at any other time, on the arrival of a guest
whom they desire greatly to honour, like Abraham
in entertaining his angel visitants, kill a sheep, lamb,
or kid of the goats, for the wealthiest now would
seldom venture on so valuable an offering as the fat
young calf prepared by Israel's hospitable and generous ancestor. The entire animal is cooking hard
by in the great iron pot before you have been an
hour in your host's tent. But in this case, when
the joints appear whole, they are ready to fall to
pieces from excessive stewing, so that each guest
easily carves for himself with his own fingers.

[1] Acts x. 13.

Thus it has naturally come about that food in Palestine consists very largely of broths and pottages, answering somewhat to our plain soups, in which the meat is served up in shreds. The poor particularly relish these soups, and in making them they use not only garden vegetables, but a great variety of wild plants. This is the chief dish at their principal or evening meal. The main nourishment is in most cases in the broth itself, which always forms the most substantial and palatable part of prepared food at a truly Oriental board. Jacob's mess of pottage, probably, from its being called " that red," the delicious Eastern preparation of red lentil soup, represented to the hungry and reckless Esau as substantial a dish as our roast beef![1] The wretched weakness and folly of Esau in being tempted by such a repast as we should understand by " a mess of pottage," has appeared no doubt to many utterly unaccountable. But what has been said above will show that this reckless, worldly-minded, famishing man had a stronger inducement to indulge his appetite ·than is generally supposed.

The liquid character of prepared food is particularly noticeable amongst the nomad population of Palestine. The usual fare of the *Bedaween* Arabs, called *ayesh*, is flour made into a paste, and boiled

---

[1] Genesis xxv. 29–34. In verse 34 it is called " lentile pottage."

with sour camel's-milk.   The latter is sometimes
exchanged for *lĕbĕn*, or goat's sour butter-milk, in
which float on special occasions the meagre pieces
of overdone meat.   It is exceedingly interesting
to observe that the forty-second Psalm bears every
mark of being written by David during a time of
exile, when he was compelled to hide in the wilderness of Judea, and live like the desert tribes.   Hence
the royal Psalmist could not, under the circumstances,
have used a more striking and appropriate metaphor.

Throughout Egypt and Syria a special kind of
jewellery is made, fashioned from gold or silver
mixed with the least possible alloy.   In Egypt
women wear plain bracelets of two thick solid
twists of such gold, with scarcely any workmanship,
but worth from twenty to thirty pounds, their value
consisting alone of the weight of precious metal
which they contain.   Though these ornaments are
solid, and of considerable thickness, they require no
clasp.   So malleable is the gold, owing to its freedom
from admixture with any other metal, that the
ends of these stout coils easily admit of being
unbent by a lady's fingers so as to be placed round
the wrist, and when in that position can with the
simple pressure of the hand be restored to their
circular form.   Gold and silver ornaments of such

kind do not, it is true, exhibit any highly-wrought work, being in too soft a state to admit of this. But, since in Bible lands massive worth seems always in trinkets to have been more highly prized than fineness of graving, this is of little consequence. There is a regular standard or assay of gold and silver jewellery of this sort, and in both cases these metals are mixed with so little alloy that they are always said to be " pure." Thus, when buying any article in the metal-worker's bazaar at Cairo, the modern capital of Egypt, the purchaser before doing so carries it to a certain officer, who is stationed on the spot, and who applies tests, and, if it be genuine, gives a written certificate stating it to be of " pure gold," or "pure silver," as the case may be. Ornaments of this kind are much prized, and are only possessed by the wealthy; whereas jewellery of the ordinary description, especially silver jewellery, is worn in great abundance by all classes.

Repeated mention is made in Scripture of this " pure gold." We are told that the furniture of the Tabernacle, and afterwards of the Temple, together with the porch of the latter, was overlaid with it.[1] Solomon's royal throne was also overlaid with the same, and whereas the ordinary drinking vessels of this magnificent monarch are said to have been of

---

[1] Exodus xxv. 11, 17, 29, 31, 38; 1 Kings vii. 49, 50; 2 Chronicles iii. 4.

"gold," those of his most splendid palace, " the house of the forest of Lebanon," so called from the vast quantity of cedar employed in its construction, are specially said to have been of "pure gold." [1] This form of the precious metal is used in several passages as a figure of great excellence and value. Thus Job in his final speech declares of Divine wisdom —

"The price of wisdom is above pearls ;

Nor shall it be weighed with pure gold." [2]

Speaking of the glories of God's anointed, the Psalmist says—

"Thou hast set a crown of pure gold on his head." [3]

In that glowing figurative picture of the Holy City, New Jerusalem, coming down from God out of heaven—the last and brightest of prophetic visions —we read of that abode of the blest, "the city was pure gold," and even its broad street shone with a like splendour. [4]

It has been observed that the various species of ants which are found in Europe lie dormant during winter. They therefore neither require nor lay up food for that season. Notwithstanding the explicit statements of Scripture to the contrary, some still

[1] 2 Chronicles ix. 17, 20.   [2] Job xxviii. 18, 19.
[3] Psalm xxi. 3.   [4] Revelation xxi. 18, 21.

say it is the same in the East. On one occasion, while encamped, about the middle of March, near Tiberias, on the western shore of the Lake of Galilee, I witnessed a sight that has left no doubt in my own mind on this subject. I was walking in the immediate neighbourhood of our tents, when I noticed a line of those large black ants, some three-eighths of an inch in length, with which I had become familiar in other parts of the country. These insects were marching towards their nest, which was hidden at a distance amongst the rich wild growth. Another party were passing them empty handed on their return. Those who were making for their nest were each laden with a grain of barley, longer and larger than themselves. They managed to drag the grain with singular rapidity, and had every appearance of having been thus engaged for a length of time. The work was proceeding in the most orderly and methodical manner, every one of the immense host being loaded in a similar way. It looked like a moving multitude of barley corns.

Curious to find whence they drew their supplies, I traced the line of ants back till I found it reaching to a spot where the corn that was to form the provender for our horses had been carelessly tossed about, and lay scattered on the ground. Possibly the *mookaries*, or mule-drivers, had spilled it from their sacks, or perhaps the tethered animals, in their eagerness to devour, had jerked it out of the nose-bags with which they are fed. What was going on under my eyes was not the mere supply of the daily needs of the insect community, but the harvesting of food that was to be laid up in store against the winter. No one who had witnessed it could doubt this any more than if he had seen fieldmice in our country laying up a store of beechnuts at a time when their food is most abundant. An explanation of the matter may be found in the warmth of regions like Tiberias and the Jordan valley generally. It is highly probable that the ants there do not experience the state of torpor in which they lie throughout the long and severe season of cold in our northern latitude, and consequently have need of food during the winter months.

Hence the accuracy and beauty of that striking figure of thrift and industry given by the inspired naturalist—

> "Go to the ant, thou sluggard!
> Observe her ways, and be wise;
> Which having no governor,
> Overseer, or ruler,
> Provideth her bread in the summer,
> And gathereth her food in the harvest." [1]

---

[1] Proverbs vi. 6–8.

Again, in his enumeration of four things which are "exceeding wise," giving the same insect as one, he dwells with admiration upon this feature of its provident character—

> "The ants are a people not strong,
> Yet they prepare their food in the summer."[1]

Summer, *kayitz*,[2] is the time of summer fruits, that is, the time when most fruits ripen—from the middle of June to the middle of August. We might expect to find that they "prepare their food in the summer" for the coming winter, the Scripture season of *hhoareph*,[3] commencing in November, when all the earth becomes bare from the last of its produce being plucked off and taken away. But that they should "gather their food in the harvest, *katzeer*,"[4] the time of cutting the crop, that is, the main winter crop of wheat or barley, which takes place towards the latter end of April and during May, almost in the first hours of settled fine weather,

---

[1] Proverbs xxx. 25.   [2] קַיִץ

[3] חֹרֶף from the root חָרַף, *hharaph*, "to pluck off." Hence it comes metaphorically to mean "to strip of honour or value," "to reproach," "to blaspheme."

[4] קָצִיר from קָצַר *katzar*, "to cut or crop off." This order of the seasons, so strange to us, occurs again in the pathetic lament in Jeremiah viii. 20—

> "The harvest is past, the summer is ended;
> And we are not saved."

It is, however, perfectly natural and strictly correct as regards Palestine, where harvest precedes summer.

when a bountiful supply to continue for six months might well tempt to idle and careless indulgence, forms a never-to-be-forgotten example of moderation, prudence, energy, and forethought—truly germs of a character "exceeding wise."

The flies of Palestine are at times terribly troublesome in the warm season. There are in particular seven different kinds, which cause great annoyance. First of these may be enumerated the *Dubban balady*, or common fly of the country, resembling our common house-fly, which appears on the plains at the beginning of April, and on the mountains about the end of that month. They come in vast quantities, and their bite in hot weather causes considerable irritation. Secondly, there is the *Dubban shurran*, or the "Donkey-fly," which specially attacks this animal, and causes it much distress. Thirdly, there is the *Dubban hhail*, or common "horse-fly," a large, flat, brown insect, said by the country people to be the Donkey-fly when it has attained its full size. It is a great torment to horses and mules, settling upon them chiefly when they are heated and fatigued in very large numbers.

A fourth species is the *Dubban azrack*, or the "blue-fly," which also attacks horses and other animals, and has a very venomous sting. When bitten by it they bleed from the wound, and become

wildly infuriated. After a long journey their bellies
and fetlocks may be seen red with blood. These
flies are mostly to be met with on the hot plains,
such as the country near *Jenin*, the En-Gannim of
Scripture, on the south of the plain of Esdraelon,
called in Scripture the plain of Jezreel, and the
plains of Acre and Sharon. To guard their valuable
horses from the fierce attacks of these insects, the
Arabs use gaudy-coloured woollen trappings, consisting of an apron over the belly, with long fringes
and four huge tassels at the corners, that, swinging
below, afford some protection to the legs.   On the
Philistine plains, from time immemorial the chief
haunt of this pest, during the latter part of summer
and the season spoken of in Scripture as "heat,"[1]
that is, from the middle of August to the latter end
of October, travelling, especially in connection with
transport of goods, is only attempted at night
time.

The fifth kind is the *Namous*, the well-known
mosquito. This torment of all hot countries abounds
in the well-cultivated and well-watered districts of
Palestine. The hissing sound they emit gives warning of their approach during the day, and the natives
by long practice are able to strike them the moment
they settle upon their hands or face before they
have time to inflict their painful sting. During the
night nets can be used to keep them at a distance,

[1] Genesis viii. 22.

but practically it is a very difficult thing to escape them altogether, even in this way. They are very numerous in the lowland districts, and reach even the highest parts of the central mountains of Israel and Judah.

A sixth and still more formidable species are called *Heshes*. These are sand-flies, and are particularly active at night-time. Not only are they very numerous, and their bite extremely irritating, but they are so small that no nets can keep them away from the sleeper, and they do not, like the mosquito, give due warning of their approach. They chiefly make their appearance in the early summer, and very formidable they are at such time.

The seventh and last kind that infest the Holy Land are the much-dreaded *Barghash*, another species of sand-fly, with glistening white wings, to be met with in the hottest districts, such as Gaza, Ramleh, the neighbourhood of Tiberias, and the Jordan valley. They are specially active and irritable at mid-day in May, June, and July. They swarm on some occasions so largely that they fill the air, and one cannot eat or drink without being obliged to swallow them. At these times they reign supreme, and are a positive plague. Even the natives of Syria are tormented by them. This I cannot help thinking must have been the insect which Vinisauf describes as causing such terrible distress to the

F

crusading army under our Richard the First, when
they were marching on the maritime plains not very
far from Hebron. He says: " The army, stopping a
while there, rejoicing in the hope of speedily setting
out for Jerusalem, were assailed by a most minute
kind of fly, flying about like sparks, which they
called *Cincinellæ*. With these the whole neighbouring region round about was filled. These most
wretchedly infested the pilgrims, piercing with great
smartness the hands, necks, throats, foreheads, and
faces, and every part that was uncovered, a most
violent burning tumour following the punctures
made by them, so that all that they stung looked
like lepers." He adds, " That they could hardly
guard themselves from the most troublesome vexa-
tion by covering their heads and necks with veils."[1]
The white glistening wings of the insect I have
described, which comes out in such crowds in the
bright sun, would well account for its being compared to a " spark." It was at Ekron, in this same
Philistine country, not far from where the crusaders
met these tiny but formidable foes, that Baal-zebub,
" the Lord of flies," was formally worshipped, and
was supposed to possess the power of predicting life
or death.[2] This form of idolatry may well have
arisen from the dread these insects inspired. The
third and fourth plagues sent upon the land of

---

[1] Harmer's *Observations*, vol. iii. p. 310.   [2] 2 Kings i. 2.

Egypt have been supposed to consist, the former
of mosquitoes, and the latter of innumerable swarms
of sand-flies.[1]

The fly is employed as a figure by the prophet
Isaiah, who cries—

"Jehovah will hiss for the fly
That is in the uttermost part of the streams of Egypt."[2]

A bold metaphor, under which a distressing invasion of the country by vast hordes of Egyptians is
graphically pictured. The terror of such a judgment may well appear from what has been said of
the nature of the flies of Palestine. The connection,
too, of gnats and sand-flies with the numerous
"streams," or artificial canals, of Egypt, which
irrigate that verdant and garden-like land, is peculiarly appropriate, for such green water-courses
form the special breeding-grounds of these insects.

Jeremiah addressing the Philistines, against whom
he is pronouncing coming woe, exclaims—

"How long wilt thou cut thyself?"[3]

To this day may be witnessed throughout the Holy
Land the hideous sight which gave rise to the allusion. The *Derweeshes*, or *Muslim* devotees, make a
practice of cutting themselves with sharp iron darts,
pointed iron maces, and swords. This sight may be

[1] Exodus viii. 16-24.　[2] Isaiah vii. 18.　[3] Jeremiah xlvii. 5.

seen in public on certain great occasions when some
so-called holy sheikh, or some celebrated pilgrim
on his journey to Mecca, makes his entry into a
city. The most devout, or rather I should say the
most fanatical, *Derweeshes* who may be present at
such time, appear stripped naked to their waist, and
transfix their cheeks, arms, and breasts with the
various weapons they carry, but more especially
with their short slender iron darts, and spiked iron
maces with dagger-like appendages at either end.
The holes in their flesh into which these instruments
are darted, and from which they may afterwards be
seen hanging down, have in most instances been
pierced before, and have healed over, like those
which are made for ear-rings. Sometimes these
holes in the cheeks are skilfully concealed beneath
their beards. But on other occasions, when their
feelings are wrought up to a greater pitch of frenzy,
they will seize their swords, and, first carefully
covering themselves with long sheets, will gash
their foreheads till the blood spurts out upon them!
All these exercises are professedly the effects of
anguish arising from a sense of sin, an anguish
which, in some instances, we cannot doubt to be
genuine.

These men, who abound in Palestine, are the
modern representatives of those priests of Baal,
who, during the sacrifice at Carmel, in deep distress

of mind when no fire fell in answer to their prayers, "cut themselves after their manner with swords and spears till the blood gushed out upon them."[1] In our Bibles it is said they cut themselves "with knives and lancets." The Hebrew words are *hherev*,[2] and *roamahh*.[3] *Hherev*, rendered in our version "knife," is in almost every instance (and it occurs three hundred and ninety times) rendered "sword." The word *roamahh* is in all the other fourteen passages where it occurs plainly "spear" or "javelin." The reader will observe that the correct rendering, which no doubt appeared too bold for our translators to adopt, brings out a lifelike resemblance to the practices of the modern *Derweesh !*

The eighty men, who, when coming up to Gedaliah, the governor of the cities of Judah, were so cruelly and treacherously slain by the conspirator Ishmael, were in deep mourning. In describing their appearance, we are told that, in addition to having their beards shaved and their clothes rent, they had "cut themselves."[4] Again, in drawing the picture of severe and general lamentation, the same prophet says—

"Upon all hands are gashes."[5]

---

[1] 1 Kings xviii. 28.   [2] חָרֶב   [3] רֹמַח
[4] Jeremiah xli. 5.
[5] Jeremiah xlviii. 37 ; see also Jeremiah xvi. 6.

The figurative inquiry, therefore,

"How long wilt thou cut thyself?"

means, "how long wilt thou be in grievous lamen- .
tation and distress?" It is not a little striking
and appropriate that the four allusions to this
cutting, so intimately connected with mourning,
all occur in Jeremiah, the prophet of lamentation
and woe.

The almost tropical violence with which the
winter rains sometimes descend in Syria renders
travelling in certain parts during such occasions both
difficult and dangerous. At times, too, though these
occurrences are comparatively rare, there are severe
snowstorms, after which the snow melts with great
suddenness. As much as half an inch of rain has
been known to fall within the space of half an hour
upon lands which were already so steeped with
water that no more could sink into the soil. Let
this quantity be calculated over the wide area of
the bare hillsides, and the sudden and alarming
nature of the floods which then visit a land, suffering at other seasons rather from a lack of water,
may well be understood. Lieutenant Conder, R.E.,
speaking of *Bedaween* life, says: "In more than
one instance, a sudden thunderstorm in the hills
has brought a flood down the great valleys, in the

bottom of which the smaller groups of tents are often found, and the water has carried away and drowned the whole settlement, together with its flocks."[1] Just such a scene must have been present to our Saviour's imagination when He pictured the fall of the house built on the sand during a violent winter tempest.[2]

Nor are these terribly sudden freshets the only peril of floods. Travellers in Syria, who pass through the country on ordinary occasions, can form no idea of the fury possessed during storms by streams which at other times are comparatively small. There are only about half-a-dozen bridges in the whole of Palestine, in addition to a few ferries on the Jordan. All rivers have, therefore, to be forded, either on foot or on horseback. Some, like "that ancient river, the river Kishon," are specially dangerous owing to their muddy and treacherous bottoms. Along the whole of the western coast it is usual to cross the streams at their mouths, close to the sea, where the sand which they accumulate makes them shallower. This, however, in the case of heavy storms, when a strong surf is on the beach, adds a new peril to the passage.

I well remember on one occasion, on a journey from Beyrout, after riding all night along the sea-

---

[1] *Tent Life in Palestine*, vol. ii. p. 274.
[2] Matthew vii. 26, 27.

board, arriving alone with two guides, who knew but little of that part of the country, on the banks of the river *Aujah,* four miles north of Jaffa. It was about three o'clock on a cold morning, and the river was greatly swollen. My guides did not know where to make the passage. The first time I endeavoured to cross at the spot they indicated, my horse, struggling vainly against the torrent, turned back. I forced him in again a second time, but had a narrow escape for my life. A huge wave rolling in caught us up, and in its return well-nigh drew us out to sea. I owed it to the strength and courage of my horse that I managed to escape, and wet and shivering, still found myself standing by the bank of the river from which I had started. Here I was compelled to wait until a party of peasants, passing that way, guided me to a spot higher up, where, with the water almost over the saddle, I managed to cross in their footsteps. These men, as is usual in such cases, undressed themselves, and put their clothes in a bundle on their heads, and so walked over with the stream breast high.

On that, and on other occasions, when forced during winter to ford deep, swollen, rapid rivers, I was able to realise in all its intensity the Psalmist's picture of the persecution and sorrow under which Israel had well-nigh sunk—

"Then the waters had overwhelmed us,
The stream had gone over our soul;
Then the proud waters
Had gone over our soul."[1]

Such experiences light up with a vivid fulness
of meaning the Saviour's supplication founded on
such a scene—

"Save me, O God,
For the waters are come in unto my soul.
I sink in deep mire, where there is no standing;
I am come into depths of water, and the flood
    overfloweth me.
    .   .   .   .
Deliver me out of the mire, and let me not sink;
May I be delivered from them that hate me,
And out of the depths of waters.
Let not the flood of waters overflow me,
Neither let the deep swallow me up."[2]

Better, too, they enable us to enter into the rich
comfort and beauty of that tender promise—

"And now thus saith Jehovah, Who created thee, Jacob,

---

[1] Psalm cxxiv. 4, 5.

[2] Psalm lxix. 1, 2, 14, 15. That these are the words of the Lord
Christ appears plain from verse 9, quoted in John ii. 17—

"Zeal for thy house consumed me,"

and verse 21, quoted in Matthew xxvii. 34—

"They gave me gall for my food,
And for my thirst they gave me vinegar to drink,"

which are evidently spoken by the same person. They are a vivid
expression of that "travail of his soul," that anguish which He bore
for our sake in the day when, as our sinless substitute—

"Jehovah laid on him the iniquity of us all."

And who formed thee, Israel ;
Fear not, for I have redeemed thee,
I have called thee by thy name, thou art mine.
When thou passest through the waters, I will be with
    thee,
And through the rivers, they shall not overflow thee."[1]

The people of Palestine and the surrounding countries are, as I have already had occasion to remark, passionately fond of light. That is a thoroughly Eastern proverb which says, "Truly the light is sweet," and an equally characteristic Oriental metaphor that puts "light" for joy and gladness.[2] Even poor people keep a tiny oil lamp burning all night. This practice is universal, and they are greatly surprised at the darkness which reigns in our houses at night-time after the family has retired to rest. When, therefore, the Psalmist, recounting God's mercies towards Israel, says, that at the Exodus He led them—

"All the night with the light of fire,"[3]

he not only describes a miraculous means of guidance, but one which to an Eastern nation was full of peculiar comfort. Hence in the East the possession of a light came to signify the continuance of life, for as long as a man was living he kept a

---

[1] Isaiah xliii. 1, 2.   [2] Ecclesiastes xi. 7 ; Esther viii. 16.
[3] Psalm lxxviii. 14.

lamp burning.   So Job declares of the hypocrite's destruction—

> "Yea, the light of the wicked shall be put out,
>
> The light shall become dark in his tent,
> And his lamp over him shall go out."[1]

And again—

> "How often is the lamp of the wicked put out?
> And their destruction cometh upon them?"[2]

The wise man, speaking of retributive justice, says—

> "The light of the righteous shall rejoice;
> But the lamp of the wicked shall be put out."[3]

If in the East a lamp is out at night, it must be because the house is empty and the occupant gone. In the threatened destruction of Judah and all the nations round about at the hands of the king of Babylon, the final touch to the picture of ruin is this, " I will cause to perish from them . . . the light of the lamp."[4]   And in the judgment which is yet to come upon the mystical Babylon, described so graphically in the Revelation, it is declared, "the light of a lamp shall shine no more at all in thee."[5]

To give any one a lamp in a place came in the same way to mean to establish his house and line

---

[1] Job xviii. 5, 6.   [2] Job xxi. 17.   [3] Proverbs xiii. 9.
[4] Jeremiah xxv. 10.   [5] Revelation xviii. 23.

in that place. In the days of Jehoram, who did
evil in the sight of the Lord, as the natural consequence of having the daughter of Ahab for his wife,
we read, "Yet Jehovah would not destroy Judah,
for David his servant's sake, as he promised him
to give to him a lamp for his sons always." [1] And
again of wicked Abijam, who "walked in all the
sins of his father," it is said, "Nevertheless for
David's sake Jehovah his God *gave him a lamp in
Jerusalem,* to set up his son after him, and to
establish Jerusalem." [2]   When Ahijah the Shilonite
announced to Jeroboam that God intended to wrest
ten tribes from the hand of Solomon, and give them
to his rule, he added in the name of the Lord,
"And to his (Solomon's) son will I give one tribe,
(that is, the tribe of Benjamin, which remained
steadfast to the kingdom of Judah), that David my
servant may have *a light always before me in Jerusalem,* the city which I have chosen for myself to
put my name there." [3]   It must be borne in mind
that the city of Jerusalem, and all its northern
suburbs, stood in the territory of Benjamin.   Had
this tribe joined the ten in their revolt against the
throne of Solomon, the royal city could not have
remained, as God had promised it should, the
dwelling-place of the kings of David's line; that
is, in the highly figurative language of Bible lands,

[1] 2 Kings viii. 19.   [2] 1 Kings xv. 4.   [3] 1 Kings xi. 36.

their lamp in the Holy City would have been put out.

A striking winter feature of Bethany, the modern *El 'Azariyeh*, is a number of almond trees, which cluster round the poor ruined village, leafless as yet, but beginning to put forth, early in February, an abundance of whitish blossoms largely tinged with pink. I have often admired this little grove, and whilst doing so have felt that in the solemn and affecting description of the closing scene of life—the seventh age of man—given us in the last chapter of Ecclesiastes, this tree cannot have been introduced to picture the whiteness of an old head. This light cheerful rose-colour displays far more the bloom of youth than the snows of age. It is difficult to understand why our translators here render *na-atz*[1] by the word "flourish," seeing that this Hebrew term means in every other place "to provoke," "abhor," or ".despise." It is here in the *hiphel* mood, the mood which implies "causing," and the right rendering would naturally seem to be "the almond" (that is its nut, which is throughout the Holy Land a very favourite and constant article of food) "causes loathing, and the locust" (which others can eat) "is a burden" to the aged, toothless old man.[2] The previous verses, it is true,

---

[1] יִנְאָץ   [2] Ecclesiastes xii. 5.

contain a series of figures; but at this fifth verse
there is a change, and what is there stated is a sad
literal account of nature's decay.

Well may the poetic Eastern fancy have viewed
this early active tree as nature's vigilant "watcher."
Shakaid[1] is its Hebrew name, from the root
shakad,[2] "to wake" or "watch." While the other
trees are still lifeless and bare, the almond has long
woke up from the sleep of winter, and looked
round, as it were, for the yet dormant growth of
the new year. The fact of this tree's still lingering
in a neighbourhood where so little wood is now
left seems to show that it was once very plentiful
there. The prophet, who lived at Anathoth, the
modern *Anata*, only some four miles north of
Bethany, was therefore in all probability familiar
enough with the symbol employed, when he heard
the words, "Jeremiah, what seest thou?" and
replied, "I see a branch of an almond (or watcher)
tree." He would well understand the significant
words which immediately followed, when the Lord
said, "Thou hast well seen: for I will watch over
my word to perform it."[3] The rendering in our
version is, "I will hasten my word to perform it."
There appears, however, no idea of haste intended
at all, but rather the thought of a vigilance which
points to waiting. And this, it will be seen, pre-

---

[1] שָׁקֵד   [2] שָׁקַד   [3] Jeremiah i. 11, 12.

serves the striking play upon the words "watcher-tree" and "watch," which are respectively the substantive and verbal form of the same root.

How wonderful is the patience of God! Many willingly ignorant mistake the Lord's long-suffering for slackness. But He who is Divine Patience and Divine Truth ceaselessly watches over His word to perform it in due season. Therefore it is that not "one jot or one tittle," that is, one *yod*,[1] the smallest Hebrew character, or even so much as one of the still smaller fine upturned strokes, "tittles," or rather "little horns," which distinguish some of the Hebrew consonants,[2] shall pass away till all has been literally fulfilled.[3] The golden candlestick of the Tabernacle, like Aaron's rod, exhibited in each of its branches flower, fruit, and stem of the almond.[4] Type as this sacred vessel was of the Church of the first-born, may not these ornaments have prefigured God's watchful care over the Written Word, the oracles of grace, committed to the keeping of the Church, which, notwithstanding that Church's un-

---

[1] ‎י, the Hebrew letter *yod*, or *i*, pronounced *ē*.

[2] The κεραια, *keraia*, "tittle," or rather "little horn," may be seen in the tiny turn on the left-hand top corner of the ‎ד, *daleth*, or Hebrew letter *d*, by the height of which it is distinguished from the ‎ר, resh, or Hebrew letter *r*. Three of these "little horns" occur on ‎שׁ, or *sh*, called *shin*, and they are found on many other Hebrew letters.

[3] Matthew v. 18.   [4] Exodus xxv. 31-35.

faithfulness, He has so marvellously preserved, and so unfailingly accomplished ?

There is a common belief amongst the towns-people and villagers of Palestine, and the *Bedaween* of the surrounding deserts, that hidden treasures exist underground in numerous places, and many spend much of their time in seeking to discover them. Sometimes incantations are used for this purpose. So rooted is this belief amongst all classes of people, that whenever they see Europeans engaged in the exploration of the country or its ruins, they conclude at once that the explorers are seeking for buried wealth, and nothing will persuade them to the contrary. This is one of the great hindrances to scientific researches in Syria, rendering them always difficult, and often dangerous. It greatly impeded the recent Ordnance Survey.

No doubt the universal traditions which exist as to hidden treasures rest on a good foundation. In all parts of Syria the produce of the land is stored up in a kind of underground cistern, called a *silloh*, generally in the form of a huge jar. Such secret places are scattered here and there in the "field," or open cultivated plain, and are carefully concealed from strangers. Ten out of the eighty men whom Ishmael the conspirator sought to slay, escaped by promising to reveal the spots where they possessed such buried treasure. "Do not kill us," they cried, "for we have hidden stores in the field, of wheat, and of barley, and of oil, and of honey."[1] Had death or foreign captivity overtaken them suddenly, here might have been ten sources of hidden treasure in the region of Shechem, Shiloh, and Samaria, to be found some day by others. It was certainly a common practice to deposit large sums of money at the conclusion of their funeral rites in the tombs of kings and nobles, which accounts for the careful sealing of such sepulchres by means of huge rolling-stones and other ingenious apparatus.

It seems, too, that on many occasions besides funerals, and in many places besides tombs, it was usual to bury considerable wealth. Repeatedly of late hidden treasures of this kind have been brought to light. A large number of gold Alexanders were recently discovered at Tyre. A quantity of genuine silver skekels were found in the neighbourhood of Jericho during the winter of 1873. At Haifa many Byzantine coins were found under the sill of a doorway in the gardens. During the exploration of the ruin in Jerusalem known as the *Mauristan*, which now belongs to the Emperor of Germany, a pot of gold coins was discovered. It will be seen from this how natural was the conduct of the

[1] Jeremiah xli. 8.

wicked and slothful servant in the Parable of the Talents, who, in order to put the sum he had received in a safe place, "went and digged in the earth, and hid his lord's money."[1] Thus, too, we find that Achan only adopted the usual hiding-place when stowing away "the goodly robe of Shinar" and the silver and gold, which he had coveted and stolen from the doomed spoil of Jericho. In his confession he said, "Behold, they are hidden in the earth in the midst of my tent, and the silver under it."[2]

It would appear also from recent finds that such sums of money were constantly buried in common earthenware jars, the better to aid in their concealment. May there not be an allusion to this custom when the Apostle Paul, speaking of the grace of God in the believer, says, "We have this treasure in earthen vessels"?[3] May it not be also that when he speaks of Christ as He "in whom are hidden all the treasures of wisdom and knowledge," the Apostle is contrasting, under the same bold and familiar figure, the weak human body which He took upon Him at His incarnation, with the mighty wisdom and power of the secret indwelling fulness of the Godhead?[4] To the eye of the natural man that "body of humiliation," like an earthen jar, entirely concealed the hidden treasure of Deity

---

[1] Matthew xxv. 18.   [2] Joshua vii. 21, 22.
[3] 2 Corinthians iv. 7.   [4] Colossians ii. 3.

so that to such an one He appeared only as "the son of Joseph," "the carpenter" of Nazareth, or at best as John the Baptist, Elijah, or one of the prophets.

Possibly it is with reference to the universal importance attached to the subject of buried treasure that the promise to Cyrus of wealth and prosperity runs—

> "I will give thee the treasures of darkness,
> And hidden riches of secret places." [1]

It is certain that such is the bold figure used by Job when he speaks of the miserable and bitter in soul as those—

> "Who long for death, but it cometh not;
> And dig for it more than for hidden treasures." [2]

Solomon, too, uses the same comparison when speaking of that sincere and eager pursuit of heavenly wisdom which never fails of its reward—

> "If thou seekest her like silver,
> And searchest for her as for hidden treasures:
> Then shalt thou understand the fear of Jehovah,
> And find the knowledge of God." [3]

There is scarcely one good road throughout the length and breadth of Palestine. Travellers, as they manage to pass their horses with difficulty along the wretched highways, or choose some

---

[1] Isaiah xlv. 3.   [2] Job iii. 21.   [3] Proverbs ii. 4, 5.

adjacent path over the open plain as far preferable
to the road itself, often wonder whence come the
huge rough stones, which so constantly obstruct
the way.   I was at a great loss to account for the
presence of these, until my attention was called, by
Mr. Schick, our able architect at Jerusalem, to the
manner in which many of them are brought there.
The camel, horse, and mule drivers, when they find
the burdens they have arranged on the backs of
their sumpter animals are not equally poised, instead
of rearranging them, have a cruel and senseless
custom of seizing any large stone which comes to
hand, and placing it on that side where the weight
is deficient.   This stone in time jolts off, and is
replaced by another, and often by a third and a
fourth, and in any case at the journey's end, or
when the animals are unloaded, is left where it
falls in the midst of the way.   Besides this, in
clearing the vineyards, gardens, and arable lands,
stones are constantly thrown out on to the nearest
road.

None of the highways, moreover, are at any time
properly metalled, and in winter they suffer very
severely from the tropical torrents of rain.   Neither
is there any adequate provision for keeping them
in permanent order even if they were efficiently
made.   This condition of the highways causes very
serious inconvenience in a land where every journey

has to be made on horseback, or on foot. Matters were not so bad in the time of those master road-makers, the Romans, but it is very doubtful whether the highways were ever in much better order under purely Jewish rulers. The whole character and institutions of the despotic East make against the proper preservation of works of this kind which benefit the community at large.

An intensely interesting papyrus has been found in Egypt, dating, it is supposed, about the fourteenth century before Christ, that is, as far back as the time of Israel under the Judges, probably the period of their oppression by Jabin, king of Canaan. It gives an account of the adventures of the first traveller in Palestine of whose complete tour we have any record. This gentleman was an Egyptian officer, called a *Mohar*, a man evidently of some importance, and he is represented as travelling in an iron chariot. His journey begins at Aleppo, and he visits a town near the shores of the Sea of Galilee, where a meeting has been arranged with other *Mohars*. Thence by the Jordan valley he travels to Bethshan and to Megiddo, which has been identified during the work of the survey of Western Palestine with the important ruin of *Mujedda*, and goes up its *bik'ah*, or deep cleft between the hills. Next he goes to En-Gannim, *Jenin*, through the *aimek*, or broad plain, of Jezreel, and passing Dothan

by the road along which the Midianites bore Joseph
into Egypt, he crosses the pass, now called *Wady
Mussin*, and descends into the plain of Sharon. After
an enforced stay at Joppa, he returns by an inland road
at the foot of the Judean hills to his own country.
A reference to the graphic account of this ancient
traveller will show how remarkably similar were
the incidents of a journey in Palestine two thousand
five hundred years ago to those of the present day.
As long as the *Mohar* kept to the plains, which he
appears to have done during the greater part of the
way, he seems to have managed to proceed tolerably
well; but no sooner do we find him on a mountain
road, at the pass of *Wady Mussin*, even though that
road appears to have been the long-established
caravan route into Egypt, than he tells us he
finds the way full of "rocks and rolling-stones,"
"obstructed by hollies, prickly pear, aloes, and
bushes called jackal-shoes." His horses take fright,
the pole of his carriage becomes broken, and in a
pitiable plight he manages with difficulty to reach
Jaffa some twenty-five miles away on the plain.[1]

Even in the palmy days of Solomon, Josephus
tells us as an instance of his extraordinary magnificence, that he "did not neglect the care of the
ways, but he laid a causeway of black stone [most
probably the hard, black basalt stone of the country]

[1] *Records of the Past*, vol. ii. pp. 107-116.

along the roads that led to Jerusalem, which was the royal city, both to render them easy for travellers, and to manifest the grandeur of his riches and government." [1] From the mention of these roads in the immediate vicinity of the capital as a very remarkable affair, we may gather that the other roads were not in a very different state from that in which we find them now.

Yet, notwithstanding the almost impassable condition of the highways at ordinary times, I have repeatedly observed that on a few occasions for brief intervals they were carefully mended. These few occasions were those of the arrivals of some royal personages. As soon as it was known at Jerusalem that a king or prince of the blood was about to come through any of the adjacent parts of Palestine which lie within that pashalic, orders were forthwith issued to the people of the various towns and villages to put all the roads in order over which it was arranged he should pass. This was done as usual by means of enforced labour, as was probably the case in former times. I remember once having to ride, with Dr. Chaplin, from Jerusalem to Shechem (*Nablous*), a distance of forty miles, just before one of the Russian Grand-dukes was expected to come that way, and finding, to my great surprise and comfort, that the road, generally

[1] *Antiquities of the Jews*, book viii. chap. vii. sec. 4. '

in such a state as to make any bye-path preferable, was now perfectly smooth and in order throughout. The stones had been gathered out, the broken-down embankments had been cast up, and the shelving and slippery ledges of rock on the brinks of precipices had been covered with a thin coat of earth.

Hence the proclamation in Isaiah—

"Pass ye, pass ye through the gates,
Prepare ye the way of the people ;
Cast up, cast up the highway, clear away the stones,
Lift up a standard for the peoples.
Behold Jehovah hath proclaimed unto the end of
the world :
Say ye to the daughter of Zion,
Behold, thy salvation cometh !
Behold, his reward is with him,
And his recompense is before him."[1]

Here the coming of Christ is foretold, and the preparation for the Advent of Israel's Divine King commanded, under the striking figure of the usual orders issued to make ready the highway for a royal procession. The Gentile nations are directed to pass out of the gates of their cities in order to remove all obstacles from His way, and to prepare the road of the Lord and make His paths straight, by repentance and faith,—a repentance and faith specially evidenced by kindness towards His ancient

[1] Isaiah lxii. 10, 11.

people Israel. Residents in Jerusalem of late years
have had several excellent opportunities of observ-
ing the prophet's allusion, and have learned to look
forward eagerly to the coming of some royal visitor,
if for no other reason, on account of the great
improvements immediately made in the roads upon
which he is about to travel.

Amongst the many ancient and interesting
customs that still linger in the villages of the
land of Israel, is one that may be witnessed in
those years when the harvest is bountiful, and
the tax-farmer not too rapacious. It consists of a
feast called in Arabic a *kawad*, that is, " a gathering
held at a holy place." This feast, which is regarded
as a thank-offering for a good harvest, occurs at the
time when the grain produced by the winter crop
of wheat and barley has all been gathered in and
stored away. It is given by the chief farmers of
the village, who join together for this purpose, and
invite all the inhabitants of the place, rich and
poor, and any stranger that may chance to be
amongst them. The *Imam*, or Mohammedan village
priest, whose position answers somewhat to that of
the Levite amongst the Israelites, occupies a chief
seat on such occasions, and the feast is held at a
Mukam, or " sacred place," on some hill-top, either
at the tomb of a *Wely*, or Mohammedan saint,

or under a sacred tree. A considerable number of sheep, and sometimes even one or two oxen, are roasted and eaten. This feast is accompanied by singing, and native dances conducted entirely by men, and part of the festivities consist in the giving away of wheat and other grains to the poor. It is a time of very great and general rejoicing. Mr. Samuel Bergheim, who has had seven years' experience of farming at *Abou Shousheh*, the ancient Gezer, has recently given an interesting account of this annual feast, and observes that it is "falling into disuse on account of the poverty of the peasant." [1] It would seem that to scenes such as these the prophet Isaiah refers when speaking of the gladness brought by the Advent of Christ, in the first instance to Galilee of the nations, and afterwards to all the land of Israel. He cries—

> " Thou multipliest the nation,
> Thou dost increase the joy for it :
> They joy before thee, according to the
> joy in harvest." [2]

When life has been taken in any of the frequent encounters amongst the Palestine *fellahheen,* a blood-

---

[1] *Agriculture in Palestine,* pp. 664 and 724, *Sunday at Home* for 1879.

[2] Isaiah ix. 3. The translation given above adopts a reading of the Hebrew text to be found in the margin of our Bibles, and one which the whole context of the passage seems to require.

feud arises, in which the nearest relative, as
"avenger of blood," is bound by the customary law
of the land to take the slayer's life.   In some cases
a blood fine, *Deeyeh*, is taken in lieu of life, which
amounts to 4000 piastres, or about £35, for a
man, and half that amount for a woman.   When
this is not paid, and even in many cases when it
is, their sense of honour requires the taking of a
life for a life.   The *Thâr*, or "blood-revenge," is
binding upon the relatives of the murdered person
to the fifth degree of consanguinity.   Hence
fugitives are constantly to be found who are
seeking to escape from avengers of blood, and in
need of a refuge.   This is only to be had now,
in the absence of cities of refuge, by claiming
the privilege of "sanctuary."   It may be done in
three ways.   First, by flying to a mosque, or to a
Mukam.   Secondly, by escaping to the house of
some neutral person, who rarely is known to
refuse the protection and shelter of his roof in
such a case, and who would be for ever disgraced
if he did.   The open door of such a house once
passed is invariably respected, and many lives are
saved in this way, the fugitive remaining as the
guest of the host he has thus taken by storm until
such time as matters have been sufficiently settled
to enable him to leave without risk.

There is, however, a third method of taking

sanctuary, which in all probability existed like the others in ancient times. A man when run down may save himself at the very last by calling out, " I am the *Dahheel* of (that is, one who has entered the dwelling of) such an one," mentioning the name of some person of power or rank. According to their custom, the protection of the person invoked is gained by thus merely calling upon his name. It is held to be as though the fugitive had succeeded in entering the tents or dwelling of the person he mentions. In such a case, if the avengers of blood refuse to listen to the appeal, and take the man-slayer's life, the person on whose name he has called is bound, by their code of honour, to take swift and summary vengeance. When they are in the act of killing him, the fugitive turns to some one who is present, and cries, "*Ana dahheel fulan, el amāneh andak,*"—"I am the *Dahheel* of such an one—the trust is with thee." By these words the dying man commits to the one he addresses the sacred duty of informing the protector who was invoked of what has taken place, and of relating how the victim was slain in despite of the respect due to his name. One so addressed is bound by every principle of religion and honour, however much he may dislike doing so, to accept and carry out this trust. To neglect to carry out an *amāneh*, or "trust," is in their estimation not only a deep

disgrace, but an unpardonable sin.   To call a man
Khayin el amäneh, "the breaker of a trust," is to
give him the vilest character that can be borne.

When tidings have been brought to the person
whose name was invoked by the victim of the
avengers of blood, he has the right of gathering
together all his friends and allies to assist him in
punishing the outrage, and establishing the honour
of his name.   With the customary cry, "Who is
on my side ?   Who "? [1] he calls upon them to join
their armed followers with his own men.   He
then marches to the place where his *Dahheel* was
slain, and has a right to take vengeance upon all
who were concerned in killing him during three
and one-third days, by putting to death all the
men, and seizing all the property.   For this act
of summary vengeance no blood-revenge or blood-
money can ever be claimed.   When the three and
one-third days are over a white flag is hoisted on a
pole or spear by the relatives of the *Dahheel* who
was put to death, in honour of his protector.   Any
of the offenders who have escaped with their lives
may now return in safety, and resume possession of
whatever is left of their property.[2]

[1] 2 Kings ix. 32.

[2] I am indebted for the above facts to a very able and interesting
article by Mrs. Finn, entitled *The Fellahheen of Palestine*, which
appeared in the *Quarterly Statement* of the Palestine Exploration
Fund, January 1879.

There would appear to be several allusions to this mode of taking sanctuary in the Scriptures of the Old Testament. Let Psalm xx. be read in this light. It is a prayer of the people for their king when he is in danger of his life. The Psalmist cries—

" The name of the God of Jacob defend thee.

　　　.　　　　.　　　　.　　　　.

Some trust in chariots, and some in horses,
But we will make mention of the name of Jehovah
　　our God." [1]

And rejoicing by anticipation in the salvation that this Name will bring, he cries, in apparent allusion to the flag that is set up to the protector's honour—

" We will rejoice in thy salvation,
And in the name of our God will we set up
　　a banner." [2]

Again, in another Psalm of David, whose adventurous life of border warfare had doubtless led him to become very familiar with matters of sanctuary, there seems a further reference to the same custom—

" Save me, O God, by thy name,
And by thy might vindicate me.

　　　.　　　　.　　　　.　　　　.

For strangers are risen up against me,
And oppressors seek after my life." [3]

---

[1] Psalm xx. 1, 7.　　[2] Psalm xx. 5.　　[3] Psalm liv. 1, 3.

Exulting in the power of Jehovah's exalted name, and the certainty of His vindicating those who appeal to it, he adds—

"Behold, God is my helper,

He will return the evil unto mine enemies;
In thy truth cut them off." [1]

But still plainer is the allusion of the wise man, when, speaking of the Divine protection, he says—

"The name of Jehovah is a strong tower,
The righteous runneth into it, and is safe." [2]

Here the believer who honours God by publicly calling upon His name, and by confessing his trust in the Most High as his defender, is represented as if he had fled into a strong place of refuge, where he finds safety from his foes. When Satan, like the avenger of blood, seeks our destruction, let us call upon the name of our great and compassionate Champion. The believing soul that in simple trust turns to the Lord Jesus and makes mention of His righteousness only; the soul that thus appeals to Christ by confessing its own helplessness and danger, and by placing itself unreservedly under His protection, shall assuredly find the help of One who is mighty to save, and who never fails to vindicate the honour of His great name.

[1] Psalm liv. 4, 5.   [2] Proverbs xviii. 10.

CHAPTER IV.

SHIVERING THE POTTER'S VESSEL.

" And its shivering shall be like the shivering of the potter's
    vessel,
That is broken in pieces unsparingly."
                —ISAIAH xxx. 14.

THAT glorious Messianic hymn, the second Psalm,
thus describes the final doom of those who oppose
the kingdom of God's dear Son—

"Thou shalt dash them in pieces like a potter's vessel."[1]

The connection in which the words occur prepares
us to expect that they would contain a very pointed
and powerful figure. Something more would seem
to be implied in the climax of this grand denunciation, than the ordinary breaking of an earthen
vessel. The allusion contained in the first member
of the verse,

"Thou shalt shepherd them with a rod of iron,"

which I have explained in a subsequent chapter,
leads us to look for another striking and familiar
image in the second. That something of a special

[1] Psalm ii. 9.

character is here referred to appears still more fully in the similar threatening in Isaiah. The passage is literally—

> "And its shivering shall be like the shivering
>   of the potter's vessel,
> That is broken in pieces unsparingly;
> So that in its breaking in pieces there shall
>   not be found a sherd
> To snatch fire from the burning,
> Or to take water out of a pit."[1]

Bearing in mind the size and strength of many potter's vessels in Palestine, it is plain that a mere dashing out of the hand upon the ground would fail to effect a "shivering" anything like this. To what then do the prophets refer?

The matter, I believe, admits of a very clear and deeply-interesting explanation. One of the most constant features of the land is the well or *beer*,[2] which, as no rain falls for six months together, and springs and streams are in many parts comparatively rare, becomes an essential adjunct to every house. In these large underground structures rain-water is collected from surface drainage, and stored for use during the year. The "Moabite stone" records an act, passed by Mesha, king of

---

[1] Isaiah xxx. 14. The word I have translated "shivering," שָׁבַר, *shever*, is identical in meaning with our verb, "to shiver," of which it is plainly the origin.

[2] בְּאֵר, *bĕair*, now pronounced in Arabic *beer*.

H

Moab, so far back as the days of Jehoshaphat, king
of Judah, directing every man to make a *beer*, or
rain-cistern, in his dwelling. The king tells us
"there were no wells (*beeroth*) in the interior of
the city in *Qarha;* and I said to all the people,
'Make you every man a well (*beer*) in his house.'" [1]
But such testimony would not be needed to establish
the great age of these huge artificial cisterns.
They abound everywhere, and many of them, in
fine preservation, mark the sites of very ancient
cities, where no other structure remains. There
are no less than thirty to be found within the
precincts of the Temple area at Jerusalem. Some
of these are of vast size, built on piers, and arched
like the crypt of a church. They are specially
numerous in the fine olive grove to the north of
the present city. This spot, as I shall have occasion to show in another chapter, must once have
been enclosed within the walls. Here they are in

---

[1] *Our Work in Palestine,* 1875, p. 255. The word *beer* is, in its
technical meaning, an underground rain-water cistern, and must be
so understood in most of the passages where it occurs in the Bible.
A "well (*beer*) of springing or living water" is sometimes mentioned (Genesis xxvi. 19, Canticle iv. 15). Such wells occur frequently in the sands of the maritime plains, but are very rare in
any part of the mountain districts. Several "*beers*" exist in Jerusalem, which receive rain-water like the rest, but are also periodi-
cally replenished from below. About five or six buckets full of
water come in between sunrise and sunset. This is supplied by the
infiltration from the limestone in which they are hewn out.

such a ruinous condition, apparently from extreme
age, that they now form a series of dangerous
pitfalls.

In addition to these wells there are many immense
artificial pools, or rain-water reservoirs, which are
often referred to in the Bible, and of which no
less than nine may now be traced in and around
Jerusalem itself.   One of these, the *Birket* [1] (or
Pool of) *Mamilla*, at the head of the valley of the
son of Hinnom on the south-west of the Holy City,
is 291 feet long by 192 feet wide.   Another, the
Birket es Sultan, just below the scarped fortress of
Jebus, at the south-west angle of the ancient wall,
is 510 feet long by 210 feet wide.   The *Birket
Yisrael*, supposed by some to be the Pool of
Bethesda, lying in a deep cutting along the north
of the Temple area, has a length of 360 feet, by a
breadth of 130 feet, and a depth of 50 feet.   The
Birket Hammâm, or Pool of the Bath, which is
situated at a little distance within the wall on the

---

[1] The Arabic *birket* would appear the same as the Hebrew
בְּרֵכָה, *běraikah*, translated "pool;" and this word is probably
derived from בָּרַךְ, *barak*, to kneel,—the place where the camels are
made to kneel down.   Special pools, or *běraikoth*, are mentioned at
Gibeon (2 Samuel ii. 13), Hebron (2 Samuel iv. 12), and Samaria
(1 Kings xxii. 38).   At Jerusalem the following pools are mentioned : The Upper Pool (2 Kings xviii. 17), the Lower Pool (Isaiah
xxii. 9), the King's Pool (Nehemiah ii. 14), the Pool of Siloah, or
Siloam (Nehemiah iii. 15, John ix. 7), the Old Pool (Isaiah xxii
11), and the Pool of Bethesda (John v. 2).

west side of the city, and which is supplied by an aqueduct from the *Mamilla* Pool, is 250 feet long by 150 feet broad. In connection with pools such as these, and also with many copious and important springs, there is throughout the country an extensive system of irrigation by means of aqueducts, such as I have already described, some of which are still in use, while many more lie in ruins. Josephus mentions an aqueduct twenty-five miles long, made by Pontius Pilate, the governor of Judea, in order to supply Jerusalem with water.[1]

To all these cisterns, reservoirs, and aqueducts, whether cut in the rock, or built of rough masonry, one thing is common. To render them perfectly watertight, a peculiar cement has to be used. It is composed partly of lime and partly of a large admixture of what is called in Arabic *hhomrah*. This *hhomrah* is nothing else than broken pottery of every description, ground down generally into very small pieces, and sometimes into powder. The cement thus made answers excellently the purpose for which it is employed. Every year it grows harder, until, in the case of those wells and pools where it is presumably many hundred years old, it is as firm as the rock to which it adheres.

Hhomrah is consequently an article of daily commerce throughout the country. Its preparation

---

[1] *Antiquities of the Jews*, book xviii. chap. iii. sec. 2.

by the peasants still remains the same simple and striking sight that must always have been familiar to the dwellers in every Judean town, but especially to those who lived within the waterless precincts of Zion—waterless, that is, as to *natural supply from springs or river.* Zion's very name records a situation of drought. But on the other hand, by means of its cisterns and reservoirs, Jerusalem was amply provided with water, chiefly drawn from the winter rains collected in the *beers* by surface drainage from the flat roofs and terraces of the houses, and brought there also from distant fountains, the streams of which were conducted to the city, as we have lately ascertained, by no less than five large aqueducts. This accounts for the fact that in its various sieges, while the foe without suffered from want of water, those within the walls always had enough. Beautiful figure of the Church, dry and barren as to any natural advantages, but receiving abundantly from secret and directly heaven-drawn supplies!

The manufacture of *hhomrah* may be seen now every autumn in "the valley of the son of Hinnom." This valley commences near the modern Jaffa, or *Hhulil* Gate, skirts the present fortress on Zion, and then bending to the east, and rapidly growing deeper, at the distance of a few hundred feet suddenly narrows. Here advantage has been taken of the natural formation to construct an ancient

pool, that fills up the whole width of the rocky
bed. It is called on the maps "the lower pool of
Gihon." The Arabic name is *Birket es Sultan*, "the
Sultan's Pool." It consists of two or three different levels formed by terraces of rock. Upon the
upper terrace, on the side adjoining the city,
fellahheen are sitting on the ground in front of
small brown and parti-coloured heaps. They have
under their hands a huge stone, or rather rough
piece of rock slightly rounded, about a foot to a
foot and a half in diameter, which they push backwards and forwards over the materials of the small
mounds placed before them. These mounds consist
of broken pottery, which they have purchased in
the city, or picked up from the débris outside. Here
we may see the whole of this simple but very
effective process of shivering or crushing the
"potter's vessel." The pieces heaped upon the
rocky floor form a motley mass. The greater part are
fragments of a dull reddish-brown colour, the mark
of vessels of plebeian ware, while mingling with
these are rich glazed sherds of brightest hues
and intricate design, gay vessels of the upper
classes — a little world of pottery. There are
handles, mouths, lips, spouts, and other parts of
work, that the potter has "wrought on the wheels;"
broken "earthen bottles" of every size from the
jarar (jar), three feet high, by four in circumference,

down to the common water-bottle of the country.
The work is done in the following manner. The
labourer first "girds himself," that is, fastens his
red leather belt firmly round his waist, and thrusts
the end of his only garment, a *kamise*, or long
cotton shirt, under the belt so as to be out of
the way. Then he sits down with his naked
legs wide apart. In the space enclosed between
them he scatters some of the earthenware from
an adjacent heap, and seizing the rough rounded
stone or crusher, he rolls it backwards and forwards
over the thin layer of pottery until every piece is
pounded and broken up. In a short time the whole
heap is reduced to tiny fragments of the required
size—

> " The shivering of the potter's vessel,
> That is broken in pieces unsparingly,"

is accomplished—

> " So that in its breaking in pieces there shall
> not be found a sherd
> To snatch fire from the burning,
> Or to take water out of a pit." [1]

There is yet another remarkable passage of Scripture which gathers peculiar meaning from these
facts. In the nineteenth chapter of Jeremiah, the
Lord bids the prophet " Go and get a potter's narrow-necked bottle, and take of the elders of the

[1] Isaiah xxx. 14.

people, and of the elders of the priests; and go forth into the valley of the son of Hinnom, which is by the entry of the Pottery Gate."[1] In our version it is the "East Gate," but it should be rendered the "Potter's" or "Pottery Gate," according to Jerome and others, and as given by Gesenius in his *Hebrew Lexicon*.[2] No "East" or "Sun Gate" would lead into this valley, which lies to the south; but "Pottery Gate" in every way agrees with the context. The recent deeply interesting explorations of Mr. Maudslay, C.E., have now laid bare the magnificent scarped foundations of the original wall of Zion, at the south-west corner of the city, where it rises abruptly from the very foot of the *Birket es Sultan*.[3] In following this a little farther to the east, Lieutenant Conder, R.E., says, "A broad trench here exists, and forms in all probability an approach to a gate." That such is the case is rendered the more certain by the fact of a branch

---

[1] Jeremiah xix. 1, 2. בַּקְבֻּק, *bakbook*, which I have translated 'narrow-necked bottle," is one of those words of frequent occurrence in Hebrew, where the thing signified is indicated by the sound it makes. The ordinary small narrow-necked vessel, of one invariable pattern, now used for drinking purposes by the peasantry in every part of Palestine, makes just this gurgling sound (*bakbook*) when it is being emptied. It is *invariably a pottery vessel, of the common, coarse, dull-red earthenware.*

[2] The word translated "East," חַרְסוּת, *hharsooth*, Gesenius derives from חֶרֶשׂ, *hheres*, a potsherd, and hence "the pottery" gate.

[3] See the sketch map of Jerusalem, p. 289.

FELLAHS SHIVERING POTTERY.

of the ancient road leading to Bethlehem turning
off across the valley just opposite to the supposed
site of the gate, which would be otherwise quite
unaccountable.   This entrance to the city would
be close to the spot I have pointed out as that
where earthen vessels are crushed, and it is remarkable that the heaps of rubbish in the valley
immediately below seem to consist in greater part
of broken and very ancient pottery.   From these
heaps much of the material used for *hhomrah* is
now gathered.   It seems highly probable that future
explorations will disclose somewhere here, along the
face of the lately-discovered scarped foundation of
the southern wall, the place of a gate.   If this
conjecture proves right, it will be emphatically
the "Pottery Gate," leading to the "potter's field,"
still called Aceldama, immediately opposite, which
continued until recently to be the burialplace of
strangers, and which is one of the few spots in
the neighbourhood where the soil is of clay.

At this Pottery Gate the man of God is commanded to make a proclamation of the terrible
judgments that should be sent upon the idolatrous
city.   "Then," he is told, in verses 10 and 11,
"shalt thou shiver the narrow-necked bottle in
the sight of the men that go with thee; and thou
shalt say unto them, Thus saith Jehovah of hosts:
'Even so will I shiver this people, and this city,

*as one shivereth a potter's vessel, that cannot be
made whole again.'*" To this day, in and around
Jerusalem, there is but one spot where the work
of preparing *hhomrah*, or crushed pottery, is commonly carried on, and that is *where I have described it on the northern ledge or margin of the
pool in this same "valley of the son of Hinnom," hard
by the site of the supposed Pottery Gate!* To find the
industry again in the neighbourhood of the city it
is necessary to cross the *nahhal*, or torrent valley, of
Kidron, and visit the threshing-floor at the summit
of Olivet, where it is also sometimes to be seen. In
the East, every trade and manufacture has its own
peculiar street or locality, to which it is principally
confined. These localities are, like everything else
Oriental, stereotyped by a spirit which abhors any
kind of change. On the face of it, therefore, there
is every probability thatwhere the manufacture of
hhomrah, the shivering of pottery, took place in the
days of Jeremiah, it would be found to-day.

What a striking scene then is here presented!
The prophet, surrounded by some of the principal
men of the city, passes down to the spot where
the peasants are sitting at their humble employ.
In his hand he bears the common water-bottle of
the country. Arrived at the valley of Hinnom,
before the wondering crowd that has followed, the
man of God dashes the small earthen pitcher upon

the rocky floor, and now, girding himself like the other workmen, and seating himself upon the ground, rolls over it repeatedly a huge stone, "as one shivereth a potter's vessel that cannot be made whole again," that is, grinding it with ease in a few moments into minute fragments. Then came the solemn words, "Thus saith Jehovah of hosts: 'Even so will I shiver this people, and this city.'" Significant, never-to-be-forgotten picture of the terrible judgment of God!

When Nebuchadnezzar saw in a vision a glimpse of the history of Gentile nations until the final consummation of Messiah's kingdom, he beheld the destruction of these world-powers represented apparently under the very figure we have been considering; for he saw "till that *a stone was cut out, without hands,*" that is, a natural rough stone, "which smote the image upon its feet of iron and clay (that is, baked clay, or earthenware), and broke them to pieces;" even grinding them to powder, till they "became like chaff from the summer threshing-floors; and the wind carried them away."[1] There are, it should be noted, two kinds of *hhomrah,* or crushed pottery, which are usually prepared. The one called "thick *hhomrah*" consists of little pieces about a quarter of an inch square. The other called "thin *hhomrah,*" used principally

[1] Daniel ii. 34, 35.

for making the roofs and walls of houses water-tight, is ground into a fine dust. The striking allusion in Daniel is plainly to the preparation of the latter.

It would seem that our Blessed Saviour has referred to the same subject. When commenting apparently upon the words of the 2d Psalm—

"Thou shalt dash them in pieces like a potter's vessel,"

He speaks of Himself first as the chosen corner-stone, which unbelievers, by rejecting, may be said to stumble over; and then, by a quick but natural transition to a different but kindred figure, He tells us of another aspect of His work. With respect to those who at any time oppose His kingdom, He says, "Every one that falls upon that stone shall be broken;" and with regard to the finally impenitent, who are to be "dashed in pieces like a potter's vessel," He declares, with awful significance, in view of our subject, "But on whomsoever it shall fall, it will scatter him as the dust," that is, "grind him to powder."[1]

We do well to ponder this view of the Saviour's Advent. "Knowing therefore the fear of the Lord," says the Apostle Paul, "we persuade men."[2] The coming of Christ has two aspects. One, infinitely happy, is the relief, comfort, and glory

---

[1] Luke xx. 18.　　[2] 2 Corinthians v. 11.

of His people. They, at the first stage of His second coming, both the living and the dead, will be "caught up to meet him" when He comes into "the air," thenceforth to be for ever with Him. [1] The other, unspeakably terrible, is the destruction of an ungodly world. This will assuredly take place at His "manifestation," or "revelation," the second stage of His second coming, when, accompanied by all His risen and translated saints, He will again descend to earth. Then He will come " with the clouds (that is, with startling majesty); and every eye shall see him, and they that pierced him (the Jews—Zechariah xii. 10): and all the tribes of the earth shall wail because of him. Even so, Amen." [2] Then shall be "the revelation of the

---

[1] 1 Thessalonians iv. 13–18; Revelation xx. 4, 5, 6. Three times in His deep discourse, given in the sixth chapter of John's Gospel, Christ promises resurrection to the believer, saying with significant iteration, "I will raise him up at the last day" (John vi. 40, 44, 54; see also verse 39). Now, seeing that all men are to rise again with their bodies, unless it was some special privilege, in a word, "the first resurrection," this special promise would have no meaning. The Apostle Paul, like all the early Christians, fully understood "the blessed hope" (Titus ii. 13) contained in these words of the Saviour, and regarded it as the chief prize of the Christian calling, for he tells us it was the expectation of this that nerved him for all his sufferings and labours : "Yea verily, and I count all things to be loss . . . if by any means I may attain unto *the resurrection from the dead*" (Philippians iii. 8–11).

[2] Revelation i. 7. The Revised Version of the New Testament has "shall wail *over* him." This seems an unsatisfactory rendering of κόψονται ἐπ᾽ ἀυτὸν, *kopsontai ep auton*. People in the East only

Lord Jesus from heaven with his powerful angels in flaming fire, rendering vengeance to them that know not God, and to them that obey not the gospel of our Lord Jesus : who shall suffer punishment, [even] eternal destruction from the presence of the Lord and from his mighty glory."[1] The compassionate warnings of the Bible are full of the latter aspect of the Second Advent. In the Hebrew Scriptures there are no less than forty words which signify "to destroy." It were to be wished that the preaching of our day, especially that addressed to the careless, had caught more of the tones of Scripture on this solemn subject. With a laudable desire to set forth the love of God in all its rich fulness, there is a tendency to overlook His holiness. Much is made of mercy, but justice and judgment are often lightly passed over. Not so with the preachers of the Bible. From Enoch, the seventh from Adam, to John, the last of the prophets, they unite with one voice in loud and solemn warnings to the unconverted, and choose the most powerful figures to picture the ruin of those who continue to resist the grace of God.

"wail over" a dead body. The preposition ἐπὶ, epi, means often "because of," sometimes "before" or "in the presence of," and at others "in respect to," "concerning," or on "account of," any of which would be more correct here than "over." When the verb κόπτω, koptō, means to "wail over," the particle ἐπὶ, epi, is not used (Luke viii. 52 ; xxiii. 27).

[1] 2 Thessalonians i. 7-9.

CHAPTER V.

THE NIGHT-MIST.

" I will be as the night-mist unto Israel."
—HOSEA xiv. 5.

THE wise man, speaking of the inestimable blessing of moisture in a hot land, and tracing it to its two principal sources, namely, the storehouses of deep subterranean caverns from which springs and rivers flow, and the storehouses above of dense, vapoury clouds, says of Jehovah, as it is in our version—

" By his knowledge the depths are broken up,
And the clouds drop down the dew." [1]

---

[1] Proverbs iii. 20. The word "clouds" here, שְׁחָקִים, *shĕh-hakeem*, some would render "sky," but in most passages where it occurs in the plural, if not in all, it undoubtedly means "clouds." Where the rendering "sky" is absolutely required, as distinguished from clouds, which is only twice, it occurs in each instance in the singular. Both the passages are in Psalm lxxxix. The first is in the question of verse 6—

" Who in the sky (שַׁחַק, *shahhak*) shall be compared unto Jehovah ? "

The second is found in verse 37, where it is said of the throne of David—

" It shall be established for ever as the moon,
And as the faithful witness in the sky (*shahhak*)."

I

Here there seems plainly a mistake; and not
only captious objectors, but even earnest critics,
have found an insuperable difficulty. That "the
clouds" should "drop down the dew" is contrary
to all experience in this land, or in the neighbouring regions of Europe. On a cloudy night no dew
ever falls. The diamond drops are only deposited
during clear and absolutely unclouded weather.
The reason of this is well ascertained. Dew is
the moisture held during day by the air whilst
it is warm. If the air is rendered cooler, it is
compelled to drop some of this moisture. When
the upper part of the air is cooled, the water falls
in rain; when the lower part of the air is cooled,

In Job xxxvii. 21, *shĕhhakeem* must mean clouds, and not the clear
expanse of sky.

"And now men see not the light which is shining in the clouds (*shĕhhakeem*),
  But the wind passeth and cleareth them."

Here the idea is that of the sun's shining in, that is, amongst and
behind, the clouds, unseen by men till the wind comes, and, by
driving away the cloudy veil, reveals its light. The same rendering is required by the question in Job xxxviii. 37—

    "Who numbereth the clouds (*shĕhhakeem*) by wisdom?"

Out of the eighteen times that this word occurs in the plural, it is
used no less than fifteen times together with שָׁמַיִם, *shamayeem*.
But *shamayeem* is undoubtedly the Hebrew technical expression for
the sky, or firmamental heavens, and hence *shĕhhakeem* must have
a different meaning. The derivation of the word *shahhak* is plainly
from the root שָׁחַק, *shahhak*, "to pulverise," "to grind to powder,"
"to make into dust" (2 Samuel xxii. 43; Psalm xviii. 42), and the
connection between dust and light clouds is obvious. The word
shahhak in the singular is used in Arabic for "thin cloud."

the water gently forms as dew. At night, if the air is clear and cloudless, and only in that case, the earth cools quickly. When, in consequence of this, the surface of the ground becomes colder than the air, the latter parts with its moisture, which distils on flower, leaf, and land in sparkling drops of dew. If a cloth is laid over a bush, which keeps it warmer by preventing the escape of its heat, though all around is bright with moisture, none will be found on the covered bush. Just in the same way, when clouds are spread over the earth, they hinder its heat from escaping, the air is not cooled, and dew is not formed. These are in the West such well-known facts, that even reverent men of science have felt at a loss to find any explanation whatever for the inspired statement—

" The clouds drop down the ' dew.' "

And yet Solomon is literally and absolutely right in the positive statement which he really makes. That the word rendered " dew " in our Bible stands for something far more refreshing and valuable than the richest dew, may be gathered from a glance at its figurative use in the Bible. Speaking of the boundless power of an absolute Eastern monarch to help his friends, we read—

" His favour is as ' dew ' upon the grass."[1]

---

[1] Proverbs xix. 12. In this and the following eight quotations, I

God Himself, the King of kings, speaking of the final and consummate blessedness of His ancient people, holds out this as the promise which includes it all—

"I will be as the 'dew' unto Israel."[1]

Dying Jacob desired this blessing for his best-beloved son.

"God give thee from the 'dew' of heaven"[2]

stands first, as the sum and chief of temporal good. David, in anguish of soul at the loss of Jonathan, could utter no more terrible curse upon that fatal spot where his friend fell than this—

"Ye mountains in Gilboa !
No 'dew,' and no rain be upon you,
Nor fields of offerings ! "[3]

It is said of saved Israel's mighty influence for good during the millennium—

"And the remnant of Jacob shall be,
In the midst of many peoples,
As 'dew' from Jehovah."[4]

Many other such passages occur, and all seem

retain the word "dew," putting it in inverted commas, not because it is correct, but in order that the reader may the better recall the familiar passages.

[1] Hosea xiv. 5. [2] Genesis xxvii. 28.
[3] 2 Samuel i. 21. [4] Micah v. 7.

to indicate an excellence, which, useful and refreshing as the dew is, it certainly does not possess here, even in the driest seasons. I will now show in what this remarkable excellence consists, namely, in the very fact which seems so incredible to us, that in Palestine

" The clouds drop down the ' dew.' "

First let me say that in the winter, during fine weather, dew is deposited, as in other countries, by the cooling of the surface of the ground on cloudless nights. But, inasmuch as winter is the one period of the year when much rain falls in tropical torrents, ordinary dew, which chiefly forms at such time, is, comparatively speaking, entirely valueless. This, therefore, cannot be that peculiar and inestimable blessing so often referred to by the inspired penmen. The principal season when a provision of the nature of dew is needed in the Holy Land, and when it is so abundantly given, is in summer and autumn. Then six consecutive months of drought occur regularly, even under the most favourable circumstances. From about the first week in May to the middle of October, in the usual course, no drop of rain falls, and throughout the twelve hours of each day the sun shines with great strength, unveiled by a single cloud. In autumn the thermometer has been known to register 118° Fahrenheit in the shade on the hot plains. Although the temperature is seldom as high as this, yet, during the whole period from May to October, the power of the sun, so often alluded to in the Bible, is very great, and but for the extremely dry, salubrious, and exhilarating air, would prove véry exhausting. As it is, no Eastern cares to encounter its rays at noon. The heat and drought are also greatly intensified at intervals during the months of May and October by the *shirocco*, the burning East wind, so often alluded to in Scripture.[1]

In consequence of the continuous rainless heat, vegetation becomes much parched, and would be altogether scorched from the face of the earth but for the following beautiful provision. At such time, and more especially towards its close, in the latter part of August and during September and October, the prevalent westerly winds bring an immense quantity of moisture from the Mediterranean Sea. The watery element, with which they are charged, becomes condensed when it meets the cold night air upon the land; for it is a great peculiarity of Syria that the nights are often as cold as the days are hot, a fact which I have painfully experienced during many a long journey, and which Jacob lamented three thousand six hundred years

---

[1] Genesis xlvi. 6; Jeremiah xviii. 17; Ezekiel xvii. 10; xix. 12; Hosea xiii. 15.

ago.[1] This condensation, or cloud-forming, happens more especially when the damp winds reach the hills, over the surface of which their liberated moisture rolls in masses of dense mist, which leave everywhere in their progress an immense amount of that which answers to the " dew " of the Bible. In the strict scientific sense of the word, this is rain, and not dew at all in our meaning of the word, since the vapour becomes condensed in the air before touching the ground. It answers somewhat to the lightest form of Scotch mist, but then it must be remembered that this mist in Palestine *never occurs in the daytime, but only forms during the night,* when by radiation the earth has thrown off its heat, and the cool air above it condenses the moisture borne by the breezes from the sea. From its coming only during the hours of night, from its not falling like other rain from the upper air, but forming not far above the surface of the ground, from its separation into very fine particles and not appearing to fall in drops, from the general appearance it leaves behind, and from its effects ceasing to be seen when the sun grows hot, it was rightly held to differ so much from the nature of ordinary rain as to require to be distinguished by a special technical term, *tal,* which,

[1] "Thus I was ; in the day the drought consumed me, and the cold by night " (Genesis xxxi. 40).

fortunately for the English reader, our translators have uniformly rendered in each instance by the word "dew."[1]

Let it be borne in mind that whenever we read of "dew" in our Bible, we must not understand such dew as we have here at all, but a copious mist shedding small invisible rain, that comes in rich abundance every night about twelve o'clock P.M. in the hot weather when west or north-west winds blow, and which brings intense refreshment to all

---

[1] This Hebrew word טַל, *tal*, which occurs thirty-five times in the Old Testament, is undoubtedly derived from טָלַל, *talal*, "to cover over [as a roof]" (Nehemiah iii. 15), of which there is a Chaldee form, טְלַל, *tĕlal*, "to shadow" (Daniel iv. 9). The meaning of these is confirmed by the Arabic *talla*, "to cover," "to shade," "to be a shady day." All three roots convey the same idea, which is incompatible with that of dew in the scientific sense of the term, distilling as it does invisibly, but is exactly in keeping with those covering, shady clouds which drop down in their passage the "dew" of Scripture. It is very interesting to observe that the Greek δροσος, *drosos*, and the Latin *ros*, both of which have been hitherto rendered "dew," in their ordinary and poetical use would seem to have precisely the same signification as the Hebrew *tal*, seeing that the climates of Greece and Southern Italy are similar to that of Palestine, and that they have each the Mediterranean Sea on the west. There are two adjectives formed from the Greek word δροσος — δροσοειμων, *drosoeimōn*, and δροσερος, *droseros* — meaning respectively "dew-clad" and "dewy," both of which are used of clouds, νεφελαι, *nephelai* (Aristophanes, Nub. 338; Orphica, H. 20, 6). This word *nephelai*, from which comes through the Latin our word nebulous, means "cloud masses," and occurs in the sense of "light fleecy clouds," the very "dew" clouds I have described. We meet in the *Hippolytus Coronifer* of Euripides with the ex-

organised life. Thus the mention of "dew" in any
narrative passage, such as that of the miracle
granted to Gideon,[1] will always enable us to identify
the time of year as that of the hot season, more
especially towards its close.

Often, when on autumn mornings I have risen
before sunrise from my tent on the heights to the
west of Jerusalem, and ridden into the Holy City
to conduct our early Hebrew morning service on
Mount Zion, I have reined up my horse to gaze on

pressions δροσος κρηναια, *drosos krēnaia*, "dew from a fountain,"
and ποταμια δροσω, *potamia drosō*, "with dew from a river," where
evidently no scientific dew can be meant, but a mist, rising in the
one case from a spring, and in the other from a stream. But the
words δροσος θαλασσια, *drosos thalassia*, "dew from the sea," which
also occurs in the same play, are a still more unmistakable example
of this use, and seem to describe the very Mediterranean clouds of
night-mist such as form the "dew" of Palestine. The fact that
Aristotle in his *Meteorologia* (lib. i. cap. x.), and in his *De Mundo*
(cap. iii.) speaks of dew in its strict scientific sense, in no way
affects the question of the ordinary popular and poetic use of the
term. There is less reason to examine the meaning of the Latin
ros, as it is evidently the same as the Greek δροσος. The name of
rosemary, however, a herb which flourishes upon the mountains
around the sea-board of the Mediterranean, *ros marinus*, "the sea-
dew," given because this fragrant plant requires much moisture, is
a remarkable proof, if words mean anything, that the Latin *ros* was
applied to the night-mist borne by the breezes from the Great Sea
westward. Rosemary, like many of the other familiar members of
the sweet and wholesome *labiatæ* family, such as mint, peppermint,
lavender, majoram, sage, and thyme, flourishes luxuriantly upon
the mountains of Western Palestine, where it enjoys so richly those
copious "dews" from the sea, which gave its Latin name.

[1] Judges vi. 36–40.

a sight of wondrous beauty. Very vividly it stands
before me now. Billowy masses of silvery white
or opaline clouds roll below in fantastic, ever-
changing forms, from which the summits of the
mountains now stand out like rocky islands on a
wide chain of picturesque lakes, and now seem like
the low foot-hills of mighty snow-clad ranges
towering behind them to the sky.. The scene shifts
rapidly, as the dense masses of vapour, glistening
with all the exquisite brightness of Syrian light,
wave hither and thither, or are sucked up by the
rising sun, leaving behind them on the ground for
a few hours a delightful moisture.[1] I did not then
realise, as I do now, that I was gazing upon
what Isaiah calls "a cloud of 'dew,'" as it is
literally—

"A thick 'dew'-cloud in the heat of harvest."[2]

The peculiar features of this rich provision of
nature, by which it differs from and greatly excels

---

[1] It was to these fugitive clouds that Hosea compared Israel's
brief and transient seasons of repentance—

"Your goodness is like the morning cloud,
And like the 'dew' which early goeth away."
(Hosea vi. 4).

[2] Isaiah xviii. 4. This "*dew*"-cloud is evidently distinguished from
a *rain*-cloud, which latter is never known "in the heat of harvest."
The word used here for cloud עָב, *av*, is eight times rightly rendered "thick clouds" in our version.

any kind of dew, and comes to be of such very
great value, are threefold. First, its falling only
in the hottest and driest season, when no other
moisture is to be had. Secondly, its coming every
night during such season when west winds blow,
which they do with great regularity at this time
of the year. Thirdly, its falling so copiously as
to supply all the moisture needed for vegetation
generally. The water these low clouds deposit is
perfectly sufficient to ripen the summer crops, to
keep life in the pastures of the desert, to nourish
the fig, fatten the berry of the olive, and give to
the grape its fulness of luscious juice—in a word, to
revive and sustain all hardy forms of vegetable life.

The abundance of moisture deposited by this
"dew," far exceeding that which could possibly
come from any dew properly so-called, makes the
sign given to Gideon, though not a whit the less
miraculous, still far more natural than if dew
such as we experience was intended. That Jerub-
baal should be able to wring "the 'dew' out of
the fleece, a bowl full of water," is perfectly in
accordance with the plentiful way in which this
"dew" of the Bible still falls.[1] What intensity of
pathos, too, is thus added to the Saviour's words
of tender reproach, when He graciously represents
Himself as waiting through the night of sin and

[1] Judges vi. 38.

backsliding without the portals of His faithless
Church, saying—

<blockquote>
" Open to me,

For my head is filled with ' dew,'
And my locks with the drops of the night ! "[1]
</blockquote>

The exposure to these dense chilly clouds of mist
is a far more painful ordeal than to be kept out of
doors on a dewy night when the weather is invariably dry and still.

Bearing in mind this meaning of " dew " will
account for its being constantly associated in Scripture with rain; for it is indeed a fine shower, or
rather night-mist, beginning to fall generally about
midnight, and supplying the place of our summer
rain, but without any of the inconvenience attending the latter.   Although so much moisture is
deposited as sometimes to soak through the thick
canvas of a tent, and to leave the appearance on
the ground of a gentle shower, yet, on the other
hand, it is not enough to injure the gathered grain
crops which lie on the open-air threshing-floors
during the season of " dew."   In further quotations
I will call it by its true description, " the night-
mist."   In the grand prophetic Song of Moses,
we meet amongst its opening strains with the following highly-poetic passage, the force and beauty
of which can be but little known to the ordinary

<hr>

[1] Canticles v. 2.

English reader as he finds the translation in our version—

> " My doctrine shall gush out as the rain-shower,
> My speech shall flow as the night-mist (*tal*),
> As the soft fall upon the fresh-springing grass,
> As the heavy, copious showers upon the herbage." [1]

---

[1] Deuteronomy xxxii. 2. In our version it reads—

> " My doctrine shall drop as the rain,
> My speech shall distil as the dew,
> As the small rain upon the tender herb,
> And as the showers upon the grass."

The Hebrew word rendered " distil " in the second line, נָזַל, *nazal*, in every other passage requires the meaning of " to flow," " to pour out," and that in a moderate and gentle manner. Hence it is applied to the flowing out of spice odours (Canticles iv. 16); the pouring out of tears (Jeremiah ix. 18); and the flowing out of waters from melted snow and ice when warm winds begin to blow (Psalm cxlvii. 18). In the parallelism of this verse, the third line evidently repeats the idea of the second, and the fourth that of the first. The word " small rain," which I have rendered " soft fall," שְׂעִירִים, *sĕ'eereem*, only occurs once, and comes from a word שָׂעִיר, *sa'eer*, which has the signification of " hairy," as of a goat, hence " silken," " fleecy," or " soft." This is a very apt expression for the flow of the soft tiny rain-drops deposited by the fleecy clouds of night-mist. In the first line the word for rain is מָטָר, *matar*, which is the present Arabic colloquial term for the ordinary semi-tropical winter showers. The verb I have translated " gush out " in this same line evidently means a heavy or gushing downpour. It is derived from the root עָרַף, *'araph*, used in every instance but one with the technical sense of " to cut the throat," and hence has the idea of the gush of blood from the severed artery, a fine illustration of the strange and highly-figurative origin of many Hebrew words. The term " showers," רְבִיבִים, *rĕveeveem*, in the fourth line, is plainly derived from the root רָבַב,

In his sad lament for Saul and Jonathan, David cries—

> " Ye mountains in Gilboa !
> No night-mist and no rain be upon you."[1]

Job asks—

> " Hath the rain a father ?
> Or who begetteth the drops of night-mist ?"[2]

Again, when Elijah the Tishbite made his sudden appearance in Israel, denouncing judgment, he swore by Jehovah, " there shall not be night-mist or rain these years but according to my word."[3] In these four last passages " night-mist and rain " possess a more intimate and natural connection than " dew

---

ravav, " to be many or numerous," and רַב, *rav*, " great or large," and should be rendered " heavy copious showers," referring most appropriately to the *matar*, or ordinary deluging rain of winter, in the first line. It is interesting to observe that, as Moses' first words of promise in this beautiful prophetic song speak of a gushing downpour of rain (Deuteronomy xxxii. 2), exceedingly precious in the East, so almost his last words, in the " blessing " which follows (Deuteronomy xxxiii. 28), speak of the scarcely less estimable benefit afforded by abundant falls of night-mist during the hot season—

> " Also the heavens shall gush out night-mist."

Here the word I have translated " gush out," *'araph*, is that same exceedingly expressive and graphic term used for the violent downpour of winter rains, explained above. It is in this instance evidently applied to the *tal*, or " night-mist," by the figure of hyperbole, or exaggeration, to indicate extraordinarily copious autumn clouds of moisture.

[1] 2 Samuel i. 21.   [2] Job xxxviii. 28.   [3] 1 Kings xvii. 1.

and rain," seeing that they are really two different kinds of showers. The *matar*, or "rain," falls at all hours during winter, while the *tal*, or "night-mist," falls during the hours of darkness in summer and autumn.

Viewed in this light, what a depth of meaning, what a wealth of promise, there is in those sublime words, part of the grand charta of the endless national life of the Hebrew race—

" I will be as the night-mist unto Israel." [1]

Withered by the world's contempt, scorched by eighteen centuries of fiery persecution, and, far worse than suffering, by eighteen centuries of sin and hardened unbelief, God has still mercy in store for His ancient people. This barren soil shall yet bear again, for the copious clouds of Divine grace shall come, and Israel

" Shall grow as the crimson anemone,
And cast forth his roots as Lebanon.
His branches shall spread,
And his beauty shall be as the olive,
And his fragrance as Lebanon.
They that dwell under his shadow shall
return ;
They shall revive as the corn,
And grow as the vine :
The renown thereof shall be as the wine
of Lebanon." [2]

---

[1] Hosea xiv. 5.   [2] Hosea xiv. 5–7.

It is very striking in this connection to notice
that the "night-mist" of the hot season falls,
as I have shown, chiefly in the autumn, more
largely, perhaps, in September than in any other
month.   It was on the 10th of the "seventh
month" of the Jewish ecclesiastical year, which
answers to September, that the solemn day of atonement fell.   This day was to be kept as a fast
and season of repentance by the whole nation, a
day on which publicly "to afflict their souls," followed five days afterwards by the great annual
week of rejoicing known as the feast of Tabernacles.[1]   Now, there is a very general agreement
as to the figurative and typical meaning of the
three great Jewish festivals.   The feast of Passover
prefigured the death of Christ, and our redemption
through His blood.   The second great feast, that of
Pentecost, has found its prophetic fulfilment in the
first outpouring of the Holy Spirit upon the Church
by the Lord Jesus, and the gathering in and offering to God of the first-fruits of the great harvest
of souls, of which it was the earnest.   But the
third and last great feast, this same feast of Tabernacles, has not yet been fulfilled in its deep prophetic sense.   It is called also "the feast of Ingathering," and evidently signifies the glorious
completion of the kingdom of heaven in Christ's

[1] Leviticus xxiii. 27-43.

millennial reign on earth. It must, as we learn from many Scriptures, be immediately preceded by Israel's repentance as a nation, and their true turning to God in Christ. Of that day it is said, "I will pour upon the house of David, and upon the inhabitants of Jerusalem, the spirit of grace and of supplications; and they shall look upon me whom they pierced: and they shall mourn for him as one mourneth for an only [son], and shall be in bitterness for him as one that is in bitterness for his firstborn."[1]

It may quicken our zeal in endeavouring to bring the Jews to a knowledge of Jesus of Nazareth, that it is for their repentance and acknowledgment of the Saviour, that the Apostle Peter tells us the second coming of Christ, and the millennial day, the "seasons of refreshing," that is, of joy and rest which Messiah was to bring when He came in glory, "the times of the restoration of all things," now tarries. When preaching to Israel in the Temple, in Solomon's Porch, he appeals to them to accept Jesus as a nation, because on this acceptance their own future and that of the world depends. "Repent ye therefore," he cries with prophetic voice, "and turn again, for the blotting out of your sins, *in order that* seasons of refreshing may come from the presence

[1] Zechariah xii. 10.

K

of the Lord; and [*in order that*] he may send forth
the Christ, who was before appointed (that is, fore-
ordained) for you, even Jesus; whom the heaven
must receive until the times of the restoration of
all things, of which God spoke by the mouth of all
his holy prophets since the world began." [1]

If words have any meaning, we must gather from
this passage, in accordance with the teaching of the
whole of the Old Testament prophets, that the manifestation of Christ at His second coming, and the
true, long-foreshadowed keeping of the great feast
of Tabernacles, or Ingathering—that is, the glorious
consummation of Messiah's kingdom on earth—
awaits the national repentance and conversion of
the Jews.

These "seasons of refreshing," or, as the word
literally means, "coolness after heat," are well set
forth under the cool, refreshing influences of the
rich life-giving clouds of moisture, which come most
abundantly at that very season of the year when
the typical feast of Tabernacles was appointed to
be held! With a beautiful depth and appropriate-

---

[1] Acts iii. 19–21. In our version this important meaning is
entirely obscured by the misrendering of the words ὅπως ἄν,
opōs an, "when," instead of "*in order that.*" ὅπως never occurs
in the sense of "when" in all the New Testament, "nor indeed,"
to use the words of Dean Alford, "with an indicative at all; and,
if it did, the addition of ἄν, and the use of a subjunctive, would
preclude it here. It can have but one sense—'in order that.'"

ness of meaning, Jehovah has declared of that glad time, which this feast was intended to foreshadow, the time of the gathering in of all the seed of Abraham—

"I will be as the night-mist unto Israel."

And here we are naturally led to glance at a passage which has much exercised the minds of critics, and of which many fanciful and varying interpretations have been suggested. Speaking of the day when Christ is to be enthroned in Zion, it is said of Israel—

"Thy people are free-will offerings in the day
  of thy power,
In holy beauties;
From the womb of the dawn
Thou hast the night-mist of thy youth."[1]

This 110th Psalm speaks plainly of Messiah as He Himself has told us.[2] It gives a view of the accomplishment of His manifested kingdom on earth, when He shall rule in the midst of His enemies, and the seat of His power will be in Zion.

---

[1] Psalm cx. 3. The word here that I have translated youth יַלְדוּת, *yaldooth*, comes from the root יָלַד, *yalad*, "to beget." It may possibly mean "birth," but seems more likely to be "childhood" or "youth."

[2] Matthew xxii. 41–45.

This is the time when "a nation (the nation of
Israel) shall be born at once," and converted, saved,
and restored to their own land, shall begin a new,
fruitful, and everlasting career of peace and glory.[1]
This doubtless is the "youth" spoken of here, the
commencement of Israel's new life, for this third
verse of the 110th Psalm applies not to the King,
but to His people.   The rich night-mists of Divine
reviving influences will be shed forth at the close of
this dispensation, and bring about this glorious and
long-foretold new birth.   The "womb of the dawn"
seems evidently a highly poetical and thoroughly
Eastern expression for the fleecy enfolding clouds
from out of which an autumn morning in Palestine
appears to emerge.   But the mist-clad autumn
morning is, as we have seen, the time typical of the
millennium shadowed forth by the glad autumn feast
of Ingathering.   It is therefore as much as to say,
the freshness of thy new birth dates and is derived

---

[1] Isaiah lxvi. 7-11. It is interesting to observe that this time of
Israel's yet future salvation, so plainly foretold throughout this
chapter, is elsewhere represented as one of universal newness of life.
It is the time of the "first resurrection," that of the "blessed
dead," "the church of the first-born," which is to precede the
millennium (Revelation xx. 4-6). It is the time of the making of
"new heavens and a new earth" (Isaiah lxvi. 22 ; lxv. 17 ; Revelation xxi. 1). It is also the time of new life for the Gentile world,
"for if," says the Apostle Paul, "the casting away of them (the
Jews) is the reconciling of the world, what will the receiving [of
them be] but life from the dead?" (Romans xi. 15).

from the dawn of "the day of the Lord," "the day of Jesus Christ," earth's seventh millennial day of Sabbath rest, after six millennial working-days of toil and sorrow. Then, and not till then, will the people of Israel as a nation be all presented as free-will offerings before the Lord, and "in holy beauties,"[1] that is, in the glorious ceremonial services

---

[1] The expression "holy beauties," in the Old Testament, when connected with the literal Zion, does not bear that abstract application which is generally supposed, but naturally applies to the magnificent ritual worship, such as that established by the law of Moses, and perfected in the days of Solomon when he had built the Temple of Jehovah at Jerusalem, and that which will be set up again amongst Israel at Messiah's second coming. A careful reading of the last nine chapters of Ezekiel, and a consideration of their orderly connection with those that immediately precede, which tell of the restoration of Israel to their own land, and their deliverance from Gentile foes, can leave no doubt that the Temple there described is to be a literal structure. That the Temple and its ritual of sacrifice are unmistakably referred to in the prophets as existing during the millennium, appears from Isaiah lx. 7, and also from Isaiah ii. 2, and Micah iv. 1, 2, in both of which latter passages "the mountain of the House," the technical Jewish term for the Temple, is represented as being established on Mount Zion "in the end of the days," that is, "the last days." Nor is it possible to confound the earthly Jerusalem of Ezekiel with the heavenly Jerusalem of John. In the earthly Jerusalem there is to be a grand temple (Ezekiel xl.-xlvi). In the heavenly Jerusalem we read, "I saw no temple therein" (Revelation xxi. 22). Again, the city of Ezekiel is to be four thousand five hundred measures square (Ezekiel xlviii. 30–35), while the figurative Zion is said to be of the enormous size of a cube of twelve thousand furlongs, or fifteen hundred miles (Revelation xxi. 16). The area of Ezekiel's Temple is to be a square of

of Ezekiel's Temple, appear every one of them in
Zion as true worshippers of the Triune Jehovah.
But from the very earliest breaking of that day

five hundred reeds, equal to some two thousand yards, a space of
more than a square mile (Ezekiel xlii. 16–20). In connection with
its worship there will be memorial sacrifices, pointing back to the
atoning work of Messiah, just as formerly there were sacrifices
pointing forward to it. These sacrifices, it is important to observe,
differ in many respects from those of the Mosaic law (compare
Ezekiel xlv. 21–25 with Numbers xxviii. 16–24, and Numbers xxix.
13–40). The feasts of the Sabbath, New Moon, Passover, and
Tabernacles, are to be kept, and also the year of Jubilee (Ezekiel
xlv. 17–25; xlvi. 16, 17). There will be no ark in this future
Temple (Jeremiah iii. 16). There will be no court of Israel as
distinct from that of the Gentiles. All the nations of the world are
to come up formally once every year to Jerusalem, at the feast of
Tabernacles, "to worship the King, Jehovah of Hosts" (Zechariah
xiv. 16–19), while pilgrims from the end of the earth will be constantly present at all the solemn Temple services (Isaiah lxvi. 23).
The nations, it would appear, will come up to Jerusalem each year
in the persons of their chosen representatives. What "holy
beauties" will then be seen in the visible worship of Jehovah, as
each year, at the feast of Tabernacles, the service led by Israel
will be responded to by countless multitudes of every kindred and
tongue ! The area of this Temple enclosure, vast as it is, will be
none too great to accommodate so mighty a congregation. In
Zephaniah we read that at this time the confusion of Babel will be
removed, and mankind will again speak with one tongue, and that
with a view to the need of this for the purpose of united Divine
worship—

> "Then will I turn to the peoples a pure language (literally
>   'a pure lip'),
> That they may all call upon the name of Jehovah,
> To serve him with one consent (literally 'with one
>   shoulder')."   (Zephaniah iii. 9.

shall commence their new life. " From the womb of dawn,"—from its very first hours,—the Spirit's influences, like a life-giving night-mist sweeping over a parched and barren soil, shall renew their youth !

CHAPTER VI.

THE ANCESTRAL STAFF.

"Jehovah will send thy strong staff out of Zion :
Rule thou in the midst of thine enemies."
—PSALM CX. 2.

A VERY short residence in Syria serves to show that the walking-stick, or staff, occupies a much more marked and important place in that land than is commonly the case with us. It is uniformly fashioned after the same patterns, and carried constantly by the same classes as a mark of distinction. You rarely meet a Jewish *rabbi* in the streets of Jerusalem without a long, stout stick, with an ornamental handle, which is considered a badge of his calling when he appears in public. Again, *Derweeshes*, or *Fakeers*, amongst the Mohammedans, are divided into four orders. The first three orders are known respectively by bearing, when abroad, a sword, a javelin, and a spontoon. The fourth, or *el Kelanee* order, is distinguished by the carrying of a small stick called the "*mohjanet*." It is about three feet long, with a straight, natural handle,

never at a right angle with the stick, but slanting
more or less obliquely across it, and made invariably of wood of the almond tree. It is the sacred
stick so often seen in the Egyptian sculptures, and
is regarded to the present day with much super-
stitious veneration. Mohammedans believe that if
a *Derweesh* strike the ground with his *mohjanet*
several times round the bed of a sick man, he will
recover. When a *Derweesh* of this order dies, his
son succeeds him, and this succession is called
"the carrying of the *mohjanet*." Besides these,
there are the peculiar rod and staff of the shepherd, which are both so constantly to be met with
in the very extensive pastoral regions in and around
the Holy Land. These facts alone are significant
in connection with the frequent and very special
allusions to staves which occur in Scripture.

There is one such rod, however, which has not
as yet been fully described, but which, if the following conclusions are sound, is particularly entitled
to notice. It is a stout staff, from five to six feet
long, often to be met with in Palestine and the
encampments of the surrounding deserts, and plays
no inconsiderable part in affairs connected with the
most primitive forms of Eastern life. The peculiarity of this staff consists in its being always the
straight bough of a tree in its *natural and undressed state*. In that part where it is constantly

held in the hand, it is sometimes, from extreme age, much worn. This, however, is the only mark of manipulation which it bears. Such a staff, though used ordinarily as a support in walking, is something more than this, for it forms one of the recognised insignia of rank and power. It marks first the hereditary and lineally descended ruler. Even where all is primitive, in the villages of Palestine, and amongst the *Bedaween* tribes of Syria and Arabia, the customs which prevail are perhaps the most ancient of which any vestige remains. Now, the elder, or head of each village, who is also the hereditary ruler of the place, carries such a staff as I have described. His father held it before him, and, unless he is deposed, it will be borne in turn by his son. The sheikh, the hereditary and lineally descended chieftain or prince of each *Bedaween* tribe, may also be seen to carry this ancestral staff, as a badge of his dignity and power. Travellers in the Arabian desert will recall the familiar sight of the venerable white-haired chieftain who has met them at the door of his tent holding such a staff. It forms one of the prized possessions of the family. At the sheikh's death, the right to carry it passes to his eldest son, who inherits it as the head of his house and tribe.

This staff also marks the priestly rank, which it appertains to equally with the princely. The *kadi,*

AN ARAB SHEIKH LEANING ON HIS STAFF.

who sits as judge in religious questions; the *mufti*, who answers amongst Mohammedans to the chief priest; and the *ullama*, or teachers of religion, who answer in like manner to the priests—all bear, in right of their office, a staff like the one described. On the occasion, not very rare of late years, of the visit of some prince or sovereign to the Holy Land, it has been a remarkable sight to see the *kadi* and *mufti* of Jerusalem accompanying the *pasha* to meet the distinguished guest, clad in their costly robes of embroidered silk, and mounted on richly-caparisoned horses, yet bearing in their hands this rude staff; and it would be inexplicable except for the reason I have now given. The use of such a staff is an institution of the country, and, like many other such simple Oriental customs, has an appropriate symbolical meaning. As the branch is the direct and natural offshoot and representative of the parent tree, so the man who owns the ancestral undressed staff, or natural bough, is regarded as the lineal offspring, and "head of the house of his father." [1] That it should have become the mark of the priest admits of an obvious explanation. In patriarchal times each head of a house appears in the character of a priest to his own family. Noah offered a sacrifice on leaving the ark, and Abraham built an altar in the places where he abode. Melchizedec, king

[1] Numbers xvii. 3 ; Joshua xxii. 14.

of Salem, according to Jewish tradition the patriarch
Shem, is another notable example. Thus the offices
of priest and patriarchal ruler were originally vested
in the same person, and when afterwards they became distinct, as each remained hereditary, they
continued to be marked in the same manner.

In consequence of these facts coming to my
knowledge, I was led to inquire whether any reference to this staff of double office is to be found
in the Bible. Now there are two words used in
Hebrew for " tribe." One of these, shaivet,[1] will
be found fully described under a notice of the
shepherd's club. Its primary meaning is a bludgeon or club, and hence the " sceptre," or mace of
power; and from this it came to mean a " tribe,"
from the sceptre borne by its chief. The other
word, which occurs more frequently, is matteh,[2]
and often requires the rendering of rod. But
what kind of rod? I answer, evidently a means
of support, a rod used as a staff, or walking stick.
Five times we have in Hebrew the metaphorical
use "matteh lehhem," "staff, or support of bread."[3]
Jacob, we read, "worshipped [leaning] upon the
top of his staff (matteh)."[4] In our Bible the
passage in the Old Testament is translated "upon

[1] שֵׁבֶט   [2] מַטֶּה
[3] Leviticus xxvi. 26 ; Psalm cv. 16 ; Ezekiel iv. 16 ; v. 16 ; xiv. 13.
[4] Genesis xlvii. 31 ; Hebrews xi. 21.

the *bed's* head." It is only a question of the
Hebrew vowel points, which were not a part of
the inspired volume. The consonants in the ancient
rolls stand alone thus, מטה, *mtth*,[1] and might be
rendered either *mittah*, " bed," or *matteh*, " staff."
The inspired quotation, however, in the eleventh
chapter of the Epistle to the Hebrews, most emphatically decides the text in favour of the latter.
Because Papists, without a shadow of reason, have
pointed to this passage in proof of the lawfulness
of image-worship, some Protestant commentators,
with mistaken zeal, have tried to defend the evident
mistranslation of Genesis xlvii. 31. Beds in the
East consist simply of a thin woollen mattress, rolled
up in the morning and put on one side, and at
night stretched out for use on the floor. Hence the
derivation of *mittah*, " bed," from *natah*, " to stretch
out."[2] They are often laid on a raised portion of
the room, generally in a recess, some two feet high
by three feet broad, called in Arabic a *mastabeh*,
which accounts for such expressions as, " Thou
shalt not *come down* from the bed on which thou
art gone up."[3] Beds or couches in palaces and
great houses are still made sometimes in connection
with bedsteads, but this is rare.[4] Jacob, in all pro-

---

[1] ט, written thus with a dot in the centre, stands for a double t.
[2] נָטָה.   [3] 2 Kings i. 4. See also Psalm cxxxii. 3.
[4] Canticles iii. 7 ; Amos vi. 4.

bability, had such a bed as David's must have been, the simple mattress we have described, for Saul commanded concerning the latter, "Bring him up to me in the bed (*mittah*)."[1] Such, too, was the bed of the paralytic man in the Gospels, which our Lord directed him to take up. It will be seen at once that it is impossible in such a case to speak of "worshipping on the bed's head."

Not only do we thus gather that the *matteh* was a staff for support, but, if we trace the word back to its primary meaning, we find it agreed that this is "branch," or "bough," from the root already mentioned, *natah*, " to stretch out," " to spread abroad."[2] Here, then, we have the idea of a natural branch used as a staff, and, since we know that *shaivet*, club, signifies tribe, from the club or sceptre borne by its chief, is it not reasonable to infer that *matteh*, bough, or natural staff, means tribe, from the undressed hereditary rod in the possession of the head of its principal family ? If this conclusion is sound, then *matteh*, as distinguished from *shaivet*, would be *a tribe as lineally descended from the patriarchs.* Now this is a shade

---

[1] 1 Samuel xix. 15. This command is rendered somewhat more reasonable than might at first sight appear by the fact that Eastern men and women, even of the highest class, never undress at night, or use any different clothing, simply removing their outer garment and their shoes before they retire to rest.

[2] Ezekiel xix. 11, 12, 14.

of meaning actually required by several passages in which it occurs, as given by Dr. Lee in his Hebrew Lexicon, namely, " a tribe peculiarly descended from the patriarchs of Israel." [1] *Shaivet* must be understood of a tribe in its federal and corporate capacity, and with regard to the sceptre or seat of power: *matteh* of a tribe viewed as a clan, represented by an hereditary chieftain.

This at once gives a new and striking significance to several passages in the Old Testament. Tamar, it will be seen, demanded from Judah one of his most valued possessions, and that by which he could be certainly identified, when, in answer to the question, "What pledge shall I give thee?" she said, " Thy signet and thy bracelets, and thy staff (*matteh*), that is in thy hand." [2] Precious as the signet, or seal, is in the East, this staff would be equally prized. Commentators have hitherto represented his daughter-in-law as a designing woman, who sought, by asking amongst other things for such a trifle as his walking-stick, to hide her object in seeking the valuable marks of identification that would be supplied by his seal and bracelets. But, if the view here taken be right, we learn that there was no attempt at deception, and have another striking touch added to the sad picture of sensual

[1] Dr. Lee refers to Numbers i. 4, 16 ; xvii. 17, 21 ; xxxi. 4, 5, &c.
[2] Genesis xxxviii. 18.

L

recklessness which must have brought upon Judah
a year of very great shame and anxiety.

We have already observed that the dying patriarch
Jacob is said to have bowed himself in worship,
leaning on the top of his *matteh*, or staff.[1] The
Apostle Paul appears to enumerate this as a special
act of faith in his letter to the Hebrews. "By
faith Jacob, when he was dying, blessed each of the
sons of Joseph; and worshipped, [leaning] upon the
top of his staff."[2] On referring to the narrative in
Genesis, the blessing the two sons of Joseph, and
the worshipping when he leaned on his staff, appear
as two entirely separate acts, which took place on
different occasions.[3] When he thus leaned upon
his ancestral staff, Jacob was taking a solemn oath
of Joseph that he would carry his remains to
Hebron, and bury him there with his fathers in the
land of promise. The act of faith, therefore, to
which allusion is so briefly but pointedly made
by the Apostle in the latter part of the verse in
the words, "And worshipped, [leaning] upon the top
of his staff," consisted in the patriarch's giving up a
splendid and honoured sepulchre, which would certainly have been his in the land of Egypt. As it
was, the officials of Pharaoh's palace, and all the
leading nobility of the country, together with an

---

[1] Genesis xlvii. 31.   [2] Hebrews xi. 21.
[3] Compare Genesis xlvii. 29–31 with Genesis xlviii.

imposing military escort, actually accompanied his coffin a distance of four or five days' journey;[1] and the state would doubtless have lavished upon him little short of royal pomp and distinction, if he had been content to be buried in their midst. Yet he gave up the extraordinary magnificence of a princely and public entombment in the greatest land of that age—an entombment, which, with its deathless monument hewn and sculptured in acres of living rock, appears to have been one of the most coveted distinctions that even that famous land could afford —to lie amongst strangers in a far-off and obscure grave. This was the act; and it was a noble expression of implicit faith in the promise of God to his fathers and to himself, that the land which held that grave would yet assuredly be theirs. Bearing these circumstances in mind, the appropriateness of the mention of this peculiar ancestral staff, and its touching and eloquent connection with the story, will be readily seen.

It is deeply interesting to observe that Jacob's choice, even from an earthly standpoint, and with a view only to the sacredness of sepulture, may be said to have been as wise as it was faithful. There is not, perhaps, one ancient tomb in all Egypt, notwithstanding the care with which such spots were formerly guarded, which has not been completely

[1] Genesis l. 7–11.

rifled, and few which do not now lie open to injury of every kind. The last resting-places of the mightiest Pharaohs are in our day shown to all comers by reckless and ignorant custodians. Yet the cave of Machpelah, which we have every reason to believe must lie under the magnificent Mohammedan mosque at Hebron, is to this hour guarded with a veneration greater than any other sepulchre has ever enjoyed! So jealously is it now watched over, that the Prince of Wales, accompanied by Dean Stanley, alone of all non-Mohammedans has been allowed to enter the mosque during this century. Only with the greatest difficulty could His Royal Highness obtain permission to visit it. A guard of two thousand soldiers had to be told off for his protection, and all the inhabitants of Hebron ordered to keep within their houses. The very name of the town in Arabic, *El Hhulil*, "the friend," commemorates the head of Jacob's family, who was "the friend of God."[1] This tomb is one of the few ancient localities in Palestine that seem to be undoubtedly genuine. For three thousand seven hundred years, Jews, Christians, and Mohammedans, amid their irreconcilable differences, have agreed in doing honour to this spot as the sepulchre of the great patriarch. Not only does the strongest tradition point to the present site being that of the

[1] 2 Chronicles xx. 7 ; Isaiah xli. 8 ; James ii. 23

actual resting-place of Abraham, Isaac, and Jacob, but also to the very building which now surmounts it, called *El Haram*, "the sanctuary," being "the workmanship of Abraham's own descendants while they yet dwelt in Palestine." The enclosure wall has been styled by Lieutenant Conder, R.E., "one of the mysteries of Palestine, and a monument inferior only to the Temple enclosure, which it resembles in style." One stone is said to be thirty-eight feet long by three and a half feet high. Lieutenant Conder remarks that "they are all drafted with the real Jewish draft, broad, shallow, and beautifully cut, as at Jerusalem."[1] The Bordeaux pilgrim who saw it A.D. 333 describes it as "a quadrangle constructed of stones of great beauty," evidently the one now existing. Benjamin of Tudela, a Jewish traveller, who visited it A.D. 1163, when it had passed into the hands of the Christians, who had named the building St. Abraham, says that in the former Mohammedan times it was a synagogue. He adds: "The Gentiles have erected six sepulchres in this place, which they pretend to be those of Abraham and Sarah, of Isaac and Rebekah, and of Jacob and Leah; the pilgrims are told that they are in the sepulchre of their fathers, and money is extorted from them. But if any Jew comes who gives an additional fee to the keeper of

[1] *Tent Life in Palestine*, vol. ii. p. 81.

the cave, an iron door is opened, which dates from
the times of our forefathers, who rest in peace, and
with a burning candle in his hands the visitor
descends into a first cave, which is empty, traverses
a second in the same state, and at last reaches a
third, which contains six sepulchres, those of Abraham, Isaac, and Jacob, and of Sarah, Rebekah, and
Leah, one opposite the other. All these sepulchres
bear inscriptions, the letters being engraved; thus,
upon that of Abraham we read, 'This is the sepulchre of our father Abraham, upon whom be peace!'
and so upon that of Isaac, and upon all the others.
You then see tubs filled with the bones of Israelites,
for unto this day it is a custom of the house of
Israel to bring hither the bones of their relicts and
of their forefathers, and to leave them there."
Making all due allowance for exaggeration and
inaccuracy in this curious account, there is much
reason to believe it is right in its main statement,
that the real tombs are in caves below the building.
Such is the gross superstition of the Mohammedans,
that, while they lay reckless hands on every other
monument, the tomb of any *wely*, or saint, is
regarded with the utmost veneration. They fear
that any profanation of such a spot would be fear-
fully avenged by the spirit of the saint. Hence the
boundless reverence they pay to sepulchre-shrines,
whilst they leave all else to ruin and decay.

Thus Jacob's faith in desiring to be buried in the cave of Machpelah, the humble grave of his fathers, in a distant, foreign, and at that time obscure land, has met with a reward even here below in the perpetual honour and inviolability that has attended his last resting-place from that day to this!

The next mention of such a staff brings us to Sinai. Moses, standing before the burning bush, and hearing his high commission to bring forth the children of Israel out of Egypt, tremblingly objects, ' But, behold, they will not believe me nor hearken to my voice. . . . And Jehovah said unto him : ' What is that in thine hand ? ' And he said : ' A staff ' " (*matteh*).[1] Whether this was actually Levi's original staff or not is uncertain, but it is afterwards repeatedly spoken of as " Aaron's staff," [2] to whom, both as the eldest son and as the priest, we have seen that the *matteh* would naturally belong. In reference to the wonders wrought by this staff in the presence of Pharaoh, it should be observed that the magicians also each carried a staff which they cast down in imitation of Aaron.[3] According to the mural paintings on Egyptian monuments, priests and other persons of rank were in those days accustomed to walk abroad with a staff from three to six feet long.[4] As the Egyptian priests were

---

[1] Exodus iv. 1, 2. [2] Exodus vii. 10, 12, 19 ; viii. 5. [3] Exodus vii. 12.
[4] Wilkinson's *Ancient Egyptians*, vol. iii. pp. 386-388.

distinguished by these sticks, it was fitting that
Moses and Aaron amongst God's priests should
carry the like insignia.   It will also be seen that
there was a peculiar appropriateness in the circumstances of the first miracle, when Aaron's "staff
swallowed up their staves."   Thus at the very
commencement of the contest between Jehovah and
the idols of Egypt, victory was declared on the side
of the Lord's priest, when his *matteh* devoured that
of Jannes and Jambres, "destroying their badge of
office, and symbolically putting an end to their
order altogether."

We again meet with this staff in that miraculous
proof of Aaron's Divine appointment to the priesthood, given in the seventeenth chapter of the Book
of Numbers.   And here the use of this same staff,
in itself, as we have seen, the badge of the priestly
office, in deciding which tribe had been chosen for
the hierarchy, becomes peculiarly striking and appropriate.   Moses is directed to take an almond-
wood staff, or *matteh*, from each one of the twelve
princes, or heads of the twelve tribes, and to write
every man's name on his staff.   Aaron's name was
to be written on another thirteenth staff, and these
were all to be laid up in the tabernacle of the congregation "before Jehovah," that is, before the testimony, or ark, that it might be determined by the
blossoming of one of the thirteen which of the

princes of the tribes the Lord had chosen to the hereditary office of high-priest.[1]   Dr. Thomson, in *The Land and the Book*, alluding to the fact that these staves were of almond wood, observes, that they were "selected for the purpose from the tree which, in its natural development, is the most expeditious of all; and not only do the blossoms appear on it suddenly, but the fruit sets at once, and appears while the flowers are yet on the tree, buds, blossoms, and almonds together on the same branch, as on this rod of Moses."   To this, which he justly remarks is according to the general economy of miracles, may now be added, that the staff's miraculous fruitfulness was in striking agreement with its state as a *natural undressed bough*, and with its being "the mighty staff" with which all the miracles of Moses and Aaron had hitherto been performed.

For, that Aaron's rod, thus laid up, was indeed no other than this same wonder-working staff with which the "signs" had been wrought in the land of Egypt, at the Red Sea, and in the subsequent desert journey, seems plain.   God, in giving Moses his first commission, said of the staff he then held in his hand, "Thou shalt take this staff (*matteh*) in thy hand, *wherewith thou shalt do signs*."[2]   It is twice called "the mighty staff," or, as it is literally

---

[1] Numbers xvii. 1-5.   [2] Exodus iv. 17.

in the strong Hebrew superlative, "the staff of
God" (*matteh ha-eloaheem*).[1]   At the miraculous
trial to ascertain whom the Lord had appointed
priest, the *matteh* taken to represent Aaron is
called "the staff of Levi,"[2] and also "the staff of
Aaron," though, in the case of the twelve princes
of the other tribes, it is only said that Moses was
to take "*a* staff."[3]   We are told, "Every one of
their princes gave him *a* staff apiece; for each
prince one, according to their fathers' houses, even
twelve staves; and the staff of Aaron was among
their staves."[4]   At the close of the trial each of
the twelve princes took back his own lifeless staff,
but Aaron's staff, that blossomed and bore fruit,
was brought again into the Holy of Holies, "before
the testimony," or ark—in other words, "before

---

[1] Exodus iv. 20; xvii. 9. This characteristic Hebrew mode of
forming a strong superlative by adding to a noun the genitive of
אֱלֹהִים, or אֵל, *eloaheem*, or *ail*, two different forms of the word
"God," occurs very frequently. Thus we read of "voices of God,"
or "mighty voices"—that is, "thunders" (Exodus ix. 28); of "a
trembling of God," or "mighty trembling"—that is, an "earth-
quake" (1 Samuel xiv. 15); of "mountains of God," or "mighty
mountains" (Psalm xxxvi. 6); and of "cedars of God," or "mighty
cedars" (Psalm lxxx. 10).   In the case, too, of proper names,
Carmel, "vineyard of God," signifies "most excellent vineyard,"
and Israel, "prince of God," is "a very great or mighty prince"
(Genesis xxxii. 28).

[2] Numbers xvii. 3.   [3] Numbers xvii. 2.
[4] Numbers xvii. 6.

Jehovah "—" for a token against the rebels." [1]   We hear of it next when God is about to work another miracle by the hand of Moses—the bringing water out of the rock at Meribah.   "Then Jehovah spake unto Moses, saying: 'Take *the* staff;'" and it is added, "Moses took the staff *from before Jehovah*, as he commanded him." [2]   Hence we may certainly infer that Aaron's staff which budded was the self-same staff of almond wood that Moses had carried to Sinai, and with which all the miracles were wrought.

It is deeply interesting to view the 110th Psalm in the light of these facts.   That this Scripture refers to Messiah we know by His own application of the first verse.   When the Pharisees, in answer to the Master's question, said that they thought Christ was David's son, Jesus said to them, "How then doth David in the spirit call him Lord, saying—

'Jehovah said unto my Lord,
Sit thou at my right hand,
Until I make thine enemies
A footstool for thy feet'?" [3]

---

[1] Numbers xvii. 10.   That "before the testimony or ark" is the same as "before Jehovah," we learn from a comparison of verses 4 and 7 of this same chapter.   In verse 4, God commanded concerning the thirteen staffs, "Thou shalt lay them up in the tent of meeting (the tabernacle) before the testimony."   In verse 7, where the fulfilment of this command is given, it is said, "and Moses laid up the staves before Jehovah."

[2] Numbers xx. 7, 9.   [3] Matthew xxii. 41-46 ; Psalm cx. 1.

That it is an important passage, in proof both
of Christ's priestly office and the change of the
Levitical law, we further gather from the use that
is made of it in the Epistle to the Hebrews.[1]
This 110th Psalm represents Messiah, by Jehovah's
appointment, both as Zion's king and Zion's priest—

> "Jehovah said unto my Lord :
> 'Sit thou at my right hand,
> Until I make thine enemies
> A footstool for thy feet.'
> Jehovah will send thy strong staff out of Zion :
> *Rule thou* in the midst of thine enemies.
>
> Jehovah hath sworn, and he will not repent ;
> *Thou art a priest* for ever,
> After the order of Melchizedec."[2]

The other kings of Judah were not priests. Uzziah
was struck with leprosy for attempting so much as
to burn incense. Of the tribe of Judah "Moses
spake nothing concerning the priesthood."[3] The
priests of Levi's line were not kings. Their juris-
diction only extended to things spiritual. But
this is the royal priest, after the similitude of
Melchizedec, the high-priest Joshua's great anti-
type, of whom it was said, "He shall sit and rule
upon his throne ; and he shall be a priest upon his

---

[1] Hebrews v. 6, 10 ; vii. 20, 21.
[2] Psalm cx. 1, 2, 4.　　　　　[3] Hebrews vii. 14.

throne." [1] Of this king-priest it is declared in the second verse of the 110th Psalm—

"Jehovah will send thy strong staff [2] out of Zion."

This figure is pregnant with meaning. In other places where Messiah's power and kingly authority is the subject in question, the word "sceptre," *shaivet*, is employed.[3] But the ancestral staff, as we have seen, marks the priest as well as the prince, and that prince one of lineal descent. It is here, therefore, most fitly said to be given to him who is described as bearing both offices, and as being the promised prince of David's direct line!

We read that this staff shall be sent "out of Zion." This carries us back to Aaron, and the way in which his authority as high-priest was manifested. His staff, laid up "before Jehovah," was brought out from the ark of the Tabernacle, blossoming and bearing almonds, instinct with Resurrection-life, indeed a "strong staff" of indisputable authority sent out of the sanctuary. So manifestly and mightily should Christ be exhibited to Israel

---

[1] Zechariah vi. 13.

[2] מַטֵּה עֻזֶּךָ, *matteh 'uzzĕkha.* These words are literally "the staff of thy strength." They form an idiom of frequent occurrence in Hebrew, to be rendered as above, just as "God of my righteousness" should be translated "my righteous God" (Psalm iv. 1).

[3] Numbers xxiv. 17 ; Psalm ii. 9, &c.

out of Jerusalem as their great High-priest, to
whose authority God would set supernatural seal!
That which answers to the miraculous proof of
Aaron's priesthood, in the case of our Saviour, is
undoubtedly His own resurrection.   By this His
Divine mission was incontrovertibly established.
He was "with power declared [to be] the Son of
God, according to the spirit of holiness, *by the
resurrection from among the dead.*"[1]   Just as the
blossoming, or coming to life, of Aaron's almond-
wood staff, was the sign of his appointment by God,
so Christ Himself, "the Branch of Jehovah," was
raised from the dead, as a testimony to His "un-
changeable priesthood."

This is the view given us by the Apostle Paul,
when adverting in the Epistle to the Hebrews to
the call of Christ as a high-priest.   Speaking of the
sacred office, he says, "No man taketh the honour
unto himself, but when he is called by God, even
as was Aaron.   Thus Christ also did not glorify
himself to be made a high-priest; but he who spoke
to him—

> 'Thou art my Son,
> To-day have I begotten thee.'"[2]

Now these words, which he quotes from the
2nd Psalm, refer, we know, to Messiah's resurrection, for the same apostle says in another place,

[1] Romans i. 4.   [2] Hebrews v. 4, 5.

"He hath raised up Jesus again; as it is also written in the 2nd Psalm—

> 'Thou art my Son,
> To-day have I begotten thee.'"[1]

Our Lord Himself says the same thing. When, upon His driving out of the Temple the sheep and oxen, and overturning the tables of the money-changers, the Jews demanded a sign to prove His authority, He said to them, "Destroy this temple, and in three days I will raise it up;" and He spake thus "of the temple of his body."[2] Twice, upon other occasions, when the Pharisees and Sadducees came and asked for a sign or miracle to establish His Messianic claims, He replied, "An evil and adulterous generation seeketh after a sign; and there shall no sign be given to it but the sign of the prophet Jonah," that is, as our Lord explains, His own resurrection from the dead on the third day.[3] This is still the one sign, the one "token against the rebels," in Israel.

Christ's ascension on high, and constant session on the Father's throne, was prefigured by the laying up of "Aaron's rod again before the testimony," that is, in the Holy of Holies, which, we are told, is a type of heaven.[4] The bringing out of the rod

---

[1] Acts xiii. 33.
[3] Matthew xii. 38-40; xvi. 4.
[2] John ii. 19, 21.
[4] Hebrews ix. 7-12.

once more " from before Jehovah," to work further
miracles, very fitly foreshadows our Lord's second
coming, amidst fresh miraculous signs, with power
and great glory.

Men have many schemes in our day for the
regeneration of the world, plans of their own
devising for putting an end to the miseries which
sin has brought both to individuals and to com-
munities. God's way, however, is different, and
has been declared plainly from the first. The eyes
of Adam's ruined children have been directed from
the days of our first parents to a Personal Re-
deemer, and all man's hopes have been declared
to rest upon His alone help. As a sinner he needs
an atonement, and Christ has therefore become his
high-priest, as head of the " family which is named
of God in heaven and earth." Himself the innocent
and all-sufficient Victim, He has offered up once for
all His own body, and by that " one offering hath
perfected for ever them that are sanctified." Nor
was His merciful work then ended. As man's
high-priest He still intercedes for man, yea, for
this purpose, " He ever liveth," and more especially
to procure for those who seek Him the gift of the
Holy Spirit. This work He carries on now unseen
in that Heaven which must receive Him " until the
times of the restoration of all things, of which God
spoke through the mouth of all his holy prophets

since the world began." [1]   But on the great day of
atonement the high-priest, after sprinkling the blood
on the mercy-seat within the veil, came out from the
Holy of Holies, and blessed the people of the Lord.
And though scoffers are crying, "Where is the promise of his coming? for from the day that the fathers
fell asleep all things continue as they were from
the beginning of the creation," He will come again,
and "his reward shall be with him."   For when
He thus comes, He will appear in His true character
as Zion's king.   He reigns even now in the hearts
of His believing people, for those who look to Him
as their Saviour serve Him as their Lord, and have
already experienced the protection of His power.
But then He will be manifested in all the pomp
and might of His mediatorial kingdom.   When the
wicked are crying "peace and safety," and setting
up the standard, soon to be raised, of universally
organised revolt, in the darkest hour of the night of
Jacob's trouble, in a moment, like the lightning's
flash, or the ubiquitous vulture's swoop from unseen
heights, He will come in the unimaginable glory of
the Father.[2]   When "his feet shall stand in that
day upon the Mount of Olives," all His ancient
people Israel shall be saved.[3]   The throne that
shall be set up at Jerusalem shall sway a ransomed

---

[1] Acts iii. 21.   [2] Matthew xxiv. 28.
[3] Zechariah xiv. 1-11 ; Romans xi. 26.

M

world, for the receiving back of the Jews shall be
to the rest of mankind as "life from the dead." [1]
International politics shall no longer vex the world
with war, for the Lord Christ will rule, "even
in the midst of his enemies," and "all dominions
shall serve and obey him." The problems of government will then be solved. Oppression, ignorance,
want, and crime shall cease, for "the saints of the
Most High shall receive the kingdom, and shall
possess the kingdom for ever;" yea, "the kingdom
and dominion and the greatness of the kingdom
under the whole heaven shall be given to the
people of the saints of the Most High." [2]

No less than this is the glorious prospect, given
us alike by Isaiah, the evangelical prophet, and
John, the prophet - evangelist, of that millennial
time when Jehovah shall fully accomplish the
sending forth of Messiah's "strong staff out of
Zion." Almost all students of the prophetic word
agree in believing that the indications of its glad
approach are now thickening around us. The Tal-
mud preserves the Jewish tradition that the present
order of the world would last just 6000 years;
2000 years without the law, 2000 years under the
law, and 2000 years under Messiah; and to this
conclusion the teachers of Israel were evidently

---

[1] Romans xi. 15.
[2] Daniel vii. 18, 27.   See also Isaiah xi. 1–9; lx.; lxii.; lxvi, &c.

led by those scriptures which represent a thousand years in God's sight as one day.[1] We are undoubtedly drawing near to the close of 6000 years of human history—earth's week of working-days—for, according to the latest and best calculations, we have reached a point within its last half century, and have much reason to believe that when the seventh thousand year dawns it will be the commencement of the long-foretold Sabbath, the rest that still remaineth for the people of God.[2] The shadows of evening are falling fast upon the day of this dispensation. Turning, therefore, from earthly

---

[1] Psalm xc. 4 ; 2 Peter iii. 8.

[2] The exact chronology of Scripture in the wisdom of God leaves two short breaks or chasms, which no ingenuity can fill up, and which prevent our calculating with certainty the age of the world. The first of these breaks is from the death of Moses to the servitude under the Midianites, containing the government of Joshua and the elders, and the interregnum that followed (Joshua xxiv. 31). The second uncertain interval is that which occurred between the death of Samson and the election of Saul, including the governments of Eli and Samuel. "From forty to sixty years," says Mr. H. Grattan Guinness in his very able work, *The Approaching End of the Age*, "comprises in all probability the range of the uncertain in the whole extent of Bible chronology." Mr. Fynes Clinton's deeply learned work on chronology, *Fasti Hellenici*, from the simple statements of Scripture, places the creation of the world four thousand one hundred and thirty-eight years before Christ, instead of four thousand and four years, as is generally supposed, and this gives us six thousand and eighteen years as the present age of the world, which, allowing for an error of forty to sixty years as above, is in all probability approximately true.

schemes, which must end in failure, let us patiently
wait for the Master's return with renewed hope
and redoubled watchfulness. The best preservative
amidst the peculiar perils and trials of the "last
days," is to be found in looking for our King, and
preparing to meet Him; our prayer that of the rapt
divine, "Lord Jesus, come quickly."

CHAPTER VII.

THE ORANGE.

"As an orange tree among the trees of the rocky-
  mountain-forest,
So is my beloved among the sons.
I sit down under his shadow with eager desire,
And his fruit is sweet to my taste."
—CANTICLES ii. 3.

To those who believe in the plenary inspiration of
Holy Scripture, each term which forms a part of the
original text is of very great interest. Immense
force or beauty will often be found to underlie a
single word in that volume which, to the spiritually-
enlightened, is at once the simplest and the deepest
of books. For this reason some knowledge of
Hebrew, and a thorough acquaintance with Palestine
life,—the peculiar products and primitive practices
of the land,—to a lover of the Bible are privileges
most important to possess, and imparting the richest
enjoyment.

Such thoughts naturally occur in considering
the above allegory. The tree there referred to,

rendered in this and in every other passage where it occurs in our version, "the apple tree," has long exercised the ingenuity of thoughtful and earnest commentators, and not without good reason. While all inspired illustrations are important, those which have been chosen by the Holy Spirit to set forth the glorious attributes of Christ may well be regarded as specially worthy of investigation. That this is a figure applied to the Lord Jesus we cannot doubt. It has always been held by the Church, both before and since His coming, that the Bridegroom of the Song of Solomon, He Whose "name is as ointment poured forth," that is, Messiah, the anointed one, is the Christ of God.[1] Truly "a greater than Solomon is here." He Whose person and work are its principal subjects, and Who, all glorious and all good, forms the central figure in every scene, if indeed Canticles be really part of the Sacred Canon, can be none other than Israel's Divine King. Doubtless He Himself thus declared, when in those discourses, to which they must have listened with so much delight, He "expounded" to His disciples "in *all* the Scriptures the things concerning Himself." Those who have loved their Lord best in every succeeding age have endorsed the saying of the ancient Jewish *rabbis*, that, if Solomon's Proverbs be likened to lead, and

[1] Canticles i. 3.

his Ecclesiastes to silver, his Song must be compared to pure gold. It is in the highest sense " the
song of songs which is Solomon's," or, to give the
full force of this strong Hebrew superlative, " the
chiefest and best of songs."

" The song that's all songs above,
    Longer, deeper, fuller, higher,
    Sweeter than the psalmist's lyre,
The breathing of nought but love ;
Love that is strong with strength divine,
Meet for thy depths, thou soul of mine !
Sought for in vain from the creature too long,
Painless, and deathless,—O beautiful song !

" Monarch hands the measures trace,
    Wisest child of mortal race,
    Shelomoh, a king of kings,
    Shelomoh, whose glory brings
    Shadow faint of fairer things.
For the burning words of bliss
Speak a fulness more than his ;
All the sweets that strew the song,
Prince of Peace, to thee belong,
Moves its kindling, melting fire
From thy heart, O King Messiah ! "

But though the just importance of the inspired
allegory which stands at the head of this chapter
has been owned as undoubtedly applying to Christ,
its difficulty has been equally felt. So little was
known from actual experience of the " fruitful trees "
of the Holy Land, and such excellent things were

said of this particular kind—things which could
apply to no one species with which we are familiar
in the north-west—that it was almost impossible
to decide the question. Dr. Kitto would have us
understand it to be the citron. Deriving the Hebrew
name *tappooahh*,[1] from *naphahh*, "to breathe," he
calls attention to the delicious and powerful fragrance that breathes from every part of the citron
tree. He also alludes to the fact that Oriental
ladies have the fruit often in their hands, or within
reach, and employ it for much the same purpose as
their western sisters would use a vinaigrette. When
the rind is slightly scraped or bruised, the perfume
is strongly given out. He might have added that
the Jews, both men and women, still make a similar
use of this fruit during the rejoicings of the feast
of Tabernacles. Each one strives to obtain a large
specimen without a single blemish, and having the
stalk adhering to it, for which, in lands like
Palestine, distant from its general cultivation, a
very high price has to be paid. Dr. Thomson
appears to be in error in stating that the citron is
"too small and straggling to make a shade," for like
most of the trees of that genus it grows to a considerable size, and is well calculated, by means of
its long stout leaves, to form a fine natural protection from the sun. He is, however, strictly right

[1] תַּפּוּחַ.

in asserting that its fruits are "so hard and indigestible that they cannot be used except when made into preserves." This, therefore, cannot be the tree whose fruit is sweet to the taste.[1]

The last-mentioned author, in his *Land and the Book*, would maintain in all its strictness the rendering of our authorised version. For this he relies on the similarity of the Arabic colloquial term for apple, *toophahh*, and the Hebrew *tappooahh*.[2] He

---

[1] Canticles ii. 3.

[2] It would certainly seem that the Arabic *toophahh* is the modern form of the word *tappooahh* in Hebrew. But there is a special reason why, in the case of the word "apple," we should not lay that stress upon the colloquial use of the present Arabic term which might reasonably be laid on such a use in the case of another word. In old English the word "apple" had a very general significance, applying indefinitely to any round fruit. The expression "apple of the eye," which occurs five times in our version, is an instance of this usage. It has been well remarked, "No word is more loosely used than this and all its equivalents in various languages. For instance, the Romans called almost every kind of globular fruit *pomum*, apples, pears, peaches, cherries, &c., not even walnuts excepted; and we ourselves speak of love-apples, earth-apples, oak-apples, and pine-apples, when we mean the tomato, the tuberous root of the bunium, the spongy excrescence which grows on the leaves and branches of the oak, or the most exquisite of all fruits, the Peruvian ananassa" (*Fairbairn's Bible Dictionary* — article *Apple*). In Latin, too, under the name *malum*, "apple," the Romans included also quinces, pomegranates, pears, and citrons; and Virgil's "*aurea mala*" were probably golden oranges. These last, far more likely than the quince, which is generally green rather than yellow, afforded "the golden apple" that Discord is described as casting on the table at the marriage of Thetis and Peleus, and which, through the award of Paris, was the fabled

speaks of but one place in the Holy Land, Askelon, as producing this fruit in perfection. If a really good native apple flourishes there, which I have not been able to ascertain, it must be about the only spot in Palestine where this is found to be the case. The best Syrian apples at Jerusalem come all the way from Damascus. They are the only eatable ones that I have met with, and though of a bright crimson and yellow colour, are small, and far inferior to ours. I never ate good apples in any part of the Holy Land, except at *Wady Urtas*, near Bethlehem, in the "watered gardens" belonging to the late Mr. Meshullam, and these were from foreign varieties freshly grafted. This experienced horticulturist assured me, as the result of his five and twenty years of fruit culture there, that the apple, when thus introduced, in a few years entirely deteriorates. The fact is plain that the heat of all southern parts of Palestine, even in the highest mountain districts, is far too great to permit of its reaching perfection. In some loftier and cooler regions on the Lebanon range it may do better; and Dr. Tristram, when describing

cause of the fall of Troy. Oranges, too, may have given rise to the legend of the golden apples which hung in the garden of the Hesperides. The very same general use of the word "apple" existed amongst the Greeks, who called an apricot an " Armenian apple," an orange "a Persian apple," and so forth.

a ride near Baalbec, shows us under what conditions
this must be sought. "It was interesting," he says,
"to notice how the change of vegetation registered
our increasing elevation. We had long since lost
the olive. Now the apricot became scarce, and the
apple took its place."

This accomplished botanist has come to "the
conviction that the apricot, *Mushmushah*, alone is
the apple of Scripture." It is true that it grows
abundantly in high parts of the country, and yields
much fruit. It flourishes, however, more especially
around Damascus, where the fine orchards consist
for the most part of apricots, and extend for a
circuit of many leagues, giving the glittering city,
to the Eastern imagination, the appearance of "a
diamond set in emeralds." No doubt in these wide
woods many fine specimens are here and there to
be found, beneath which Dr. Tristram might meet
with considerable shade. But in most instances
this tree is far from affording a good protection
from the sun, and would never be sought by a
Syrian for this purpose. The fruit, on an average
not so large as a good-sized English plum, is far
inferior to ours, and often comparatively tasteless.
It is whitish-yellow and pink, but not of a golden
hue. When dried in the sun, or made into a paste
for preservation until the winter months, it is perhaps
best. The fruit is thus prepared in large quantities

everywhere throughout the East. In its natural state it is not particularly wholesome. Under the most careful cultivation at the *Urtas* gardens it soon deteriorates, and the only really good apricots I have eaten in Jerusalem were, like the apples, from fresh foreign grafts. The climate of the greater part of Palestine is too hot and dry for both these trees, though the former suffers less than the latter. There is indeed a faint delicate scent possessed by the ripe fruit of the apricot, but little or none by its blossom or leaf.

Now, it may be asked, is there no tree answering fully to the description of the "apple" of Scripture, which, like the olive, vine, fig, and pomegranate, is thoroughly at home in, if not indigenous to, the soil? Is there no tree of this kind that flourishes commonly and luxuriantly in Palestine under perfectly congenial conditions? All who have resided for any length of time in the Holy Land will, I think, agree with the reply, that certainly there is just such a tree. The orange, in all its numerous choice varieties, is the rightful representative of the *tappooahh,* or "apple" of Scripture.

Before proceeding to the proof of this, let us distinctly inquire what are the marks by which the tree may be known. Briefly these are four: pleasant and powerful perfume; sweet and grateful fruit; foliage which affords a delightful shade; and a golden colour, which seems to refer to the fruit, or to the tree as seen covered with it. It is said of the bride in Solomon's Song—

"And the fragrance of thy nose [is] like the *tappoohheem*." [1]

Of the Bridegroom of the Church it is declared by His people—

> "As a *tappooahh* among the trees of the rocky
> mountain brushwood,
> So is my beloved among the sons.
> I sit down under his shadow with eager desire." [2]

To this it is immediately added—

> "And his fruit is sweet to my taste."

The intimation as to its colour is given in a truly Oriental proverb concerning wise and courteous speech—

> "A word spoken on its wheels
> Is like *tappoohheem* of gold in engraved work of
> silver." [3]

Now all these four requisites meet in a very high degree in the orange, and in that tree alone. It must be seen in the full luxuriance of its growth in Syria to realise its excellence. It may be met with in many "watered gardens" throughout the hill country, but its true home is on the warm

---

[1] Canticles vii. 8. *Tappoohheem* is the plural of *tappooahh*.
[2] Canticles ii. 3.   [3] Proverbs xxv. 11.

maritime plains, where it is now principally cultivated. Here, at Jaffa, the ancient Joppa, and at
Sidon, are vast orange orchards. The sandy plain
that forms the site of Jaffa, at a depth of from fifty
to eighty feet, supplies the water which is required
to irrigate the groves,—the supply appearing to
come from a wide subterranean river flowing at
this depth beneath the ground. In large orchards,
called in Arabic *bayarah*, oranges of many sorts
are extensively cultivated, interspersed with a few
lemons, citrons, pomegranates, bananas, and date-
palms, the whole forming a scene of surpassing
fertility and loveliness, which is guarded by a hedge
of the gigantic prickly pear (*Cactus ficus indica*).
This dull, light green, weird-looking hedge serves
the more to set off the dark, glossy, and abundant
foliage of the orange tree. The latter attains a
very considerable size, and its thick shining leaves
spread a secure and delightful shade. Beneath its
branches may constantly be seen the usual low cane
stools placed for the accommodation of the owner
and his friends. Of all the trees of the garden this
is the one chosen for shade. Nothing could be
more natural than the declaration—

" I sit down under his shadow with eager desire."[1]

The fruit is one of the most delicious and service-

---

[1] Canticles ii. 3.

able of all the productions of Palestine, and, while forming a nourishing article of food, is at the same time a natural preservative from fever. It is abundant as soon as the grapes are over, and lasts almost until they come again. It greatly excels the fruit received in this country from abroad, which has to be packed in an unripe condition. The varieties are well marked. The blood orange, which, when peeled, is of a deep crimson colour, is the sweetest, but the cultivation of this sort is now mostly confined to Egypt. There is one very large species, with an enormously thick rind, which attains the size of a small bread melon, an excellent fruit, which is not known in England. The orange is especially grateful in Bible lands. Like the produce of the vine it is most wholesome in its season, and may be freely eaten so long as care is taken not to drink water afterwards, for neglect of this precaution is, with any fruit in Palestine, a sure source of fever. " Abounding in malic and citric acid, the juice of the orange and its congeners is one of the most agreeable antidotes which the Creator's bounty has provided against the exhausting thirst and incipient fever of sultry climes. A settler in the torrid swamps of the Amazon will devour a dozen oranges before his morning meal, and in tropical regions such acidulous fruits are invaluable on account of their anti-febrile virtues." [1]   Only one like the poor, weary, sunburnt slave-girl in the Song of Songs, who has been exposed to the heat, and consequent thirst, of toil beneath a burning Syrian sky, can understand how sweet they are at such a time to the taste. [2]

The fragrance of its flowers is well known, but the alternate tropical rains and hot sun of a Syrian plain serve to increase it to a remarkable extent. As in most trees of this order, fruit, leaves, and flowers are alike scented, but more especially the latter.   They lend the most delicious perfume to the groves of orange, and one which is wafted to a great distance.   In certain winds it is perceived by ships off Jaffa, several miles away from the shore.   It is a singularly refreshing and reviving scent.   A consideration of this excellent property of the Scripture "apple" sheds a flood of light on a passage which would otherwise be meaning- less.   The bride in the Song of Songs, who is repre- sented as faint with excessive emotion, cries—

> "Straw me with *tappoohheem;*
> For I am faint with love." [3]

In our version the first line of this verse reads—

> "Comfort me with apples."

---

[1] *Fairbairn's Dictionary of the Bible*—article *Apple.*
[2] Canticles i. 5, 6 ; ii. 3.   [3] Canticles ii. 5.

But the rendering which I have here given is
that adopted by the Septuagint, and is the one required by the verb *raphad*, " to spread," in the only
two other passages where it occurs.[1] Now, the idea
of spreading over a bride either branch, blossom,
or fruit of the apple tree, possesses no significance
whatever. But if we supply the name of the true
tree in question, do we not see at once the appropriateness of the exclamation,

" Straw me with orange,"

or, as it is literally, " [pieces of] orange trees," for
this word applies equally to the tree and its
blossom as well as to its fruit? This is just what
is done to a bride down to the present day, and
here surely we have the natural Eastern origin of
the customary bridal wreath! It would appear that
on such occasions the orange flower was not formerly
in the East, as it now is in the West, a mere orna-
ment, but played an important part in the wedding
costume.

A difficulty has been felt in accounting for the
choice in Northern lands of an exotic flower for the
garland of a bride, and recently the question has
been asked in some horticultural journals, " Whence
has it arisen?" The answer is, that this practice

---

[1] רָפַד, see Job xvii. 13 ; xli. 30.

would seem plainly to have come with our race
from its Eastern cradle.   Mr. J. Timbs tells us,
"The use of these flowers (orange blossoms) at
bridals is said to have been derived from the
Saracens, or at least from the East, and they are
believed to have been thus employed as emblems of
fecundity."[1]   But the Word of God, as we have
shown, quite incidentally gives the true and far
more simple reason, namely, that they were employed
as affording a powerful perfume to revive the bride
from a natural faintness.   The strong refreshing perfume of the orange blossom, when newly gathered,
would appear to have led to its adoption as a bridal
adornment, not only perhaps for the crown or
wreath, but also as a beautiful and appropriate
addition to other parts of the dress.   It is so employed
in Palestine wherever it can be had at the present
time.   Thus there is provided, as it were, a natural
scent-bottle, the pungent and reviving fragrance of
which sustains the fainting spirits of the sensitive
maiden, who might otherwise be overcome with
emotion.   The great length of time during which
this tree is in flower singularly fits it for the
purpose by enabling its blossoms to be constantly
obtained.   Taking the various kinds which follow
each other in succession, it may be said to be in
bloom almost the whole twelve months.   Indeed

[1] *Things not Generally Known*, First Series, p. 119.

it is a peculiar excellence of the orange, *that leaves, flowers, and fruit continue on the tree together for the greater part of the year, so that it is constantly putting forth its fulness of leafage, fruitage, and perfume at the same time.* This remarkable feature has been noticed by Addison's *Spectator* in an interesting allegorical letter on "A Fine Garden." The writer says: "It rarely happens to find a plant vigorous enough to have, like an orange tree, at once beautiful and shining leaves, fragrant flowers, and delicious nourishing fruit." [1]

Let us remember that the words,

> "Straw me with orange,
> For I am faint with love,"

occur as an illustration of that fervour of deep affection with which the Church longs for the Heavenly Bridegroom, and with which each believing soul in some precious moments faints for the love of Jesus, and the desire that it has to depart and be with the Lord. The world may ridicule as mere enthusiasm the rich experiences of the believer; but Jehovah, Who "seeth not as man seeth," and Who "looketh on the heart," so far from counting these feelings as vain or imaginary, has written them down as real, and has chosen the boldest and choicest figures to set them forth.

[1] *Spectator*, No. 455.

The wise man tells us that

> "A word spoken on its wheels
> Is like oranges (*tappoohheem*) of gold in engraved
> work of silver." [1]

May not this verse contain an allusion to the peculiar feature of the orange, namely, its flowers and fruit continuing on the tree together throughout the whole season? The orange blossom is a brilliant white, resembling the colour of the molten silver so much employed in Oriental jewellery. As the rich ripe fruit is constantly seen peeping out amid clusters of the shining bloom, it is naturally to an Eastern imagination as "oranges of gold in engraved work of silver." This may have given rise to a custom, possibly existing in former times amongst the great, of serving the fruit in baskets of silver filagree. But it is more natural to suppose that the beauty and excellence of the flower-encircled produce, as it still hung on the tree, is that which is here used as a figure of the exceeding comeliness of a wise and gentle employment of man's unruly tongue.

The word *ophneem*, [2] "wheels," which occurs nowhere else but in the expression,

> "A word spoken on its wheels,"

---

[1] Proverbs xxv. 11. Lowth translates it "in network of silver;" it is literally "in figured work (מַשְׂכִּית *maskeeth*) of silver."

[2] אָפְנָיִם.

has been taken by some to contain the idea of
revolving as of the year, and hence the translation
of the line in our version,

"A word spoken in season."

But it is plain that here it simply means a literal
"wheel," as the similar form of the word *oaphan*[1]
does in every instance, and so our translators render
it in the margin. In this case

"A word spoken on its wheels,"

in the figurative language of the East, would seem
to imply "a smooth, graceful, courteous word." The
statement is thus brought into perfect accord with
the proverbial philosophy not only of the Scriptures,
but also of all Eastern lands at the present day.
Throughout the Orient the greatest importance is
attached to politeness and smoothness of speech, which
is exaggerated into countless customary compliments,
which pass current among people of all classes, and
involve much fulsome flattery and waste of time.
Even in a common Eastern legal document, such as
the conveyance of a house or a piece of land, after
the mention of any of the parties to the deed, there
is added, in the case of the most ordinary individuals,
"the most honourable, the boast of his community,
the light of his sect," and further epithets in the

[1] אוֹפֶן.

same strain. The cursing and abusive language which is heard side by side with this when a Syrian is angry, only serves to heighten it by the contrast. Protestant Christians in these lands have agreed in their intercourse and correspondence considerably to curtail the number of these compliments, and to do away with all that savours of exaggeration or insincerity. Still, with that depth of true wisdom, which is at once worldly-wise and heavenly-true, our attention is thus beautifully called to the pleasantness, sweetness, and profitableness of courteous and conciliatory speech.

The Apostle Paul affords a very excellent example of such tact and delicacy in the use of language, even when called upon to administer severe reproofs. It has been well said that in his inspired correspondence he mingles "good sense and good taste with good things." Thus, while most faithfully rebuking the Corinthian Church, he speaks "truth in love," and does so after such a gentle manner, and with such "wise meekness," that they are convinced and moved, and all comes happily right. They sorrow after a godly manner, and in all things approve themselves to be clear in the matter.[1]

It may be noticed, in connection with the explanation afforded by the silvery blossom, that

[1] 2 Corinthians vii. 8–11.

a similar figure has passed into an idiom in our English tongue, namely, "flowery language," and "flowers of speech." Well is it for us when, in all our intercourse with others, the golden orange of good matter is seen set off by the fair silvern flowers of a good manner! Some earnest Christians do not attach to this subject the importance it undoubtedly deserves.

The great vitality and longevity of the orange are specially worthy of remark. Its vigorous, almost unexampled life, in maintaining thick shining foliage, abundant fragrant flowers, and luscious fruit, *all at the same time,* has been already mentioned. To this it should be added that the tree is known to attain a very great age, and to continue to a late period its marvellous fecundity. In the orangery at Versailles, one tree bears the inscription, "*semé en* 1421," "sown in 1421;" while another in the yard of the convent of St. Sabina, at Rome, is said to have been planted in the year 1200. In Holland many orange trees still flourishing are said to have been in the same family for two hundred and three hundred years. Even in Europe an aged tree has been known to yield nearly eight thousand oranges a year. Well does this intense vitality fit the orange to illustrate the excellency of Him Whose earliest earthly symbol was Eden's Tree of Life, yea, Who is the Life itself—Essential Life—and

Who has come down from heaven that we, though dead in sins, might receive this life from Him, and enjoy it abundantly![1]

Some have imagined that the orange is not indigenous to the soil of Syria and the adjacent parts, and allege the fact that the colloquial Arabic name in Palestine, *bourdĭkan*, is apparently a modern corruption of the Italian, *Portugal*. But to this it may be conclusively replied that the colloquial Arabic name for carriage everywhere throughout Syria is *Carrosa*, evidently an adaptation of the Italian. Yet who can doubt that in past generations the people were familiar with chariots and wheeled vehicles, which are mentioned so often in the Bible? There is a very interesting tradition throwing light on this point, which is preserved among the *Beni Sakk'r* tribe of *Bedaween* Arabs, the largest and most powerful of those which inhabit the *Belka*, or highland of Moab. It purports to account for their first emigration from the depths of the Arabian peninsula, owing to the breaking up of the tribe's flourishing settlement by a disastrous flood. They speak most distinctly of their ancestors pursuing

---

[1] John xiv. 6; x. 10. It is not without special significance that the orange used as a figure of Christ, and the olive employed as a symbol of His Church (Romans xi. 17, 24, &c.), are both alike distinguished for vital tenacity, abundant productiveness, and length of days above all other fruit-trees.

the cultivation of the orange many ages ago. Dr. Tristram says : " There is a curious tradition relative to the *Beni Sakk'r* (Sons of the Falcon), that about twelve hundred years since they left their cradle in the centre of Arabia; that their forefathers lived there in a district very like that of *M'zab*, in the African Sahara, where there were no springs, but where the water was collected into enormous tanks by walls built across the *wadys* (valleys); and by these means gardens, palm groves, and *orange orchards* were fertilised." [1]   The orange tree is thus coupled with the palm in a passage in Joel, where they are mentioned, together with the olive, the vine, the fig, and the pomegranate, as some of the principal fruit-trees of the land.   The prophet cries—

" The oil languishes ;
.   .   .   .   .
The vine is dried up,
And the fig tree languishes ;
The pomegranate and the palm and the orange,
All the trees of the field are withered." [2]

This appears to me conclusive against the apple, which could never, in a hot country like Palestine, be thus preferred before the abundant apricot,[3] or spoken of as in any sense a representative tree.

[1] *Land of Israel,* 2nd edition, p. 493.
[2] Joel i. 10, 12.   "Oil" occurs elsewhere in Scripture for the olive or "oil tree."
[3] The apple is never dried for winter use in Palestine, while the

The original home of the orange was doubtless the warm lower slopes of the Himalayas, where it still grows wild, and whence it overspread Persia. But it is difficult to suppose that Solomon, who was a very eminent botanist, specially attached to the culture of watered gardens, and who, moreover, ransacked the world for the luxuries of life, failed to introduce this tree ; even if we could believe that the travelled and magnificent Egyptian monarchs had not carried it still farther west long ages before.[1] That the fruit has been familiar to dwellers in the Holy Land from very ancient times appears the more probable from the luxuriant way in which it flourishes there, in all districts where irrigation is employed, but chiefly on the hot sandy plains. The trees yield most abundantly, appearing often one mass of golden balls ; and a "*bayarah*," or orange grove, is a very remunerative property, provided only that water can be drawn up from a depth not greater than fifty or sixty feet, or, better still, furnished at a moderate royalty from some adjacent spring or stream.

Solomon, so well versed in horticulture, while

fruit of the apricot is largely prepared in this way, both whole and in the shape of apricot paste, which latter is now beginning to be imported into this country.

[1] I Kings iv. 33 ; Ecclesiastes ii. 5, 6, 8, 10 ; 2 Chronicles ix. 21–24.

laying the principal scenes of his Song in or near four different "gardens,"—that is, irrigated gardens, —if I am right, mentions the orange four times.[1] Now, the apple tree does not need irrigation, but the more delicate and juicy fruit of the orange could not live two weeks, during hot weather in the Holy Land, out of a "watered garden." The intimate and necessary association of the orange with that greatest of all refreshments in a warm country, an abundant supply of clear running water, lends it a peculiar charm, and gives an excellent coolness to its shade. I observe that a passing traveller, who speaks of her "enchanting resting-place" in an orange orchard at Jaffa, has a casual notice of this delightful feature. "Making our way," she says, "beneath the branches bowed down with their weight of golden fruit, we reached a sweet spot under the shady foliage, beside one of the rills of water flowing along the channels for the irrigation of the ground, supplied by means of a Persian wheel. It was a luxurious season of *dolce far niente*. A variety of flowers formed the carpet on which we reclined; luscious fruit hung in ripe abundance within reach of our hand; the sweet perfume of orange and lemon blossom scented the air; while the busy hum of insects (who did not torment us) mingled with the pleasantest of all

[1] Canticles ii. 3, 5; vii. 8; viii. 5.

sounds in an Eastern land, the rippling murmur of water and the soft whirr of the distant wheel." [1]

The orange is in every way a noble and excellent tree. It was not, therefore, to be supposed that it would be passed over in those Scriptures where all nature is laid under contribution to furnish the choicest figures of Christ Jesus the Lord and His redeeming work. Those who are well acquainted with its loveliness and value in a hot land will enter into something of the deep meaning of that exquisite picture of a full experience of the salvation of God—

> " As an orange tree among the trees of the rocky-
>   mountain-forest,
> So is my beloved among the sons.
> I sit down under his shadow with eager desire,
> And his fruit is sweet to my taste." [2]

How invitingly, how beautifully, is here displayed the perfect shelter of Jesus' atoning death and righteousness; the refreshing fragrance of His precious name, holy character, and all-prevailing intercession; and the satisfying sweetness enjoyed by the soul that feeds on Him, who is the true Tree of Life—the one fruitful tree in earth's wild waste!

The worth of the orange is beautifully enhanced in these verses by a striking contrast with the trees

---

[1] *Gath to the Cedars*, p. 6.   [2] Canticles ii. 3.

of the dry, tangled, rocky forests of the Judean mountains. The highly poetical comparison is—

"As an orange tree among the trees of the *ya'ar*."[1]

This is the last spot in which we should expect to find so glorious a tree. The word *ya'ar* is evidently the similar modern *wa'ar* of the *fellahheen* dialect, the technical name by which they distinguish those pathless, rocky, unenclosed, barren mountain forests, chiefly consisting of low brushwood, which form a considerable feature of the highland, or hill-country, of Palestine.

It will interest the Biblical student to trace the use of this word *ya'ar* in all the passages, some fifty-six in number, in which it occurs in the Old Testament. Upon many of these the above explanation throws a new light. Take, for instance, that where Solomon, after speaking of his "gardens and paradises, or parks," adds, "I made me pools of water, to water therewith the rocky-mountain-forest (*ya'ar*) that bringeth forth trees,"[2] that is, the rocky wilderness where he planted forest-trees, and probably arranged tiny streams, pools, and cascades, by which they were rendered cool and picturesque. To irrigate a garden or an orchard by means of artificial pools is nothing extraordinary in a land like Palestine. In the case, however,

[1] יַעַר.   [2] Ecclesiastes ii. 6.

of a mere ornamental wild, none but a very magnificent and wealthy monarch could afford such a luxurious use of water. Again, Jonathan's obtaining honey in a *ya'ar* by reaching out with "the end of the rod that was in his hand," and dipping it in the wild honey that was dropping, presumably from a rock,—for there it is that the wild swarms of bees now build, and from Scripture references appear anciently to have built,[1]—becomes at once explained by the fact that the *ya'ar* of Palestine is full of large rocks, cliffs, and caves.[2] The *ya'ar* is mentioned as a spot fatal to an army that had become entangled in it;[3] as the lair of lions[4] and bears;[5] as a lonely, deserted place;[6] as inaccessible,[7] where the words "forest (*ya'ar*) of the vintage," which have no meaning, should be "the defenced or inaccessible forest;" as a place, coupled with a desert, where it would not ordinarily be safe to sleep;[8] and as a place constantly set on fire.[9] In denouncing the chastisement of Israel, God declares of her vineyards and fig orchards—

---

[1] Deuteronomy xxxii. 13 ; Psalm lxxxi. 16.

[2] I Samuel xiv. 25–27.   [3] 2 Samuel xviii. 6–8.

[4] Jeremiah v. 6; xii. 8; Amos iii. 4.   [5] 2 Kings ii. 24.

[6] Micah vii. 14.   [7] Zechariah xi. 2.

[8] Ezekiel xxxiv. 25.

[9] Psalm lxxxiii. 14; Jeremiah xxi. 14; Isaiah ix. 18. Portions of the *wa'ar* are constantly set on fire by the charcoal burners, who often kindle in this reckless fashion a whole hillside.

" I will make them a *ya'ar*." [1]

Of the fertile mountain range to the west of the plain of Esdraelon it is said—

" Carmel shall be esteemed a *ya'ar*." [2]

Even on the once choicely cared-for Holy City, God pronounced this same doom—

" Jerusalem shall become heaps,
  And the mountain of the house (the Temple area)
    like the high places of a *ya'ar*." [3]

How literally such prophecies have been fulfilled, the neglected thickets on all these spots now attest.

The trees in the *wa'ars* are seldom large or fine, while a tangled brushwood takes up most of the dry, rock-strewn ground. Giant roots are in the soil, but that which springs from them is constantly being cut, burnt down, and kept low, owing to the great need of fuel, and the want of proper forest laws. Pleasant and fair as an orange tree would appear in any position, it would be doubly delightful in such stony, stunted woods. Thus is the glory and the goodness of Jesus mightily enhanced when we view Him beside the fairest of the sons of men, who, compared with the " chief among ten thousand," " the altogether lovely," are but as the barren " trees of the rocky-mountain-forest ! "

---

[1] Hosea ii. 12.   [2] Isaiah xxix. 17.
[3] Micah iii. 12 ; Jeremiah xxvi. 18.

" As a shining orange stands
'Mid the trees of wild waste lands,—
Where its lustrous leaves have made,
Sweet as dense, a cooling shade,
Golden pomes and silvern bloom
Ever mingle fruit and fume :
Tree of life ! whose vital power,
Fulgent leaf, fair scented flower,
Luscious fruit together bears,
Smiling thus through countless years,—
As a shining orange stands
'Mid the trees of wild waste lands,
So among earth's sons I see,
Well-beloved, no form like Thee !
Sheltered by Thy precious blood,
I recline at peace with God ;
'Neath Thy righteousness divine
Calmly rests this heart of mine,
While Thine intercessions spread
Fragrant shadow o'er my head.
Adam erst in primal glade,
Couched below the life-tree's shade,
Knowing nor to weep nor die,
Shared not such a rest as I !
More than Paradise could give
Theirs to taste on Thee who live,
Slaking fevered thirst and keen,
Sweet to me Thy fruit has been.
I shall never thirst again,
Never seek for joy in vain ;
Now by faith I feed on Thee,
Life eternal flows to me ! "

CHAPTER VIII.

THE KEEPER.

"He who keepeth thee will not slumber.
Behold, he who keepeth Israel
Doth not slumber or sleep.
Jehovah is thy keeper!"
—Psalm cxxi. 3-5.

THE infinite condescension and tenderness of God shine out brightly in every part of His word. They are, perhaps, chiefly conspicuous in those lowly human images by which He has represented His various relations towards His people. He has been graciously pleased to liken Himself to a potter, to a metal-worker or refiner, to a shepherd, to a footman or runner, and to a servant or slave.[1] A consideration of the humble nature of these occupations will prepare us for the bold metaphor by which Jehovah is pictured as the "keeper" of Israel. This representation is full of power, and would appear to refer to a custom and office peculiar to Bible lands.

[1] Romans ix. 21; Malachi iii. 3; Psalm xxiii. 1; Hebrews vi. 20; Luke xxii. 27; Philippians ii. 7.

The simple and open modes of life prevailing in the East render the services of watchmen, or keepers, of very great importance. When garden crops are ripening a keeper is hired, who, from an elevated stage, a kind of light log-hut rudely thatched with boughs of trees, guards the produce day and night. Job says of the insecurity and weakness of the wicked, in allusion to the frail temporary huts of these watchmen—

> " He buildeth his house like a moth,
> And like a booth that the keeper maketh." [1]

Vineyards must likewise partake of such care if their fruits are to be reaped. The bride in the Song of Solomon laments that this hard and menial task fell to her sad lot—

> " They made me keeper of the vineyards." [2]

Olive-yards, whose trees in one common enclosure are often owned by various proprietors, are always placed under a keeper in autumn when the fruit begins to ripen. The unlighted towns and villages, no less than the unprotected lands, render the duties of keepers, or watchmen, very arduous and important. Here they are charged to arrest any stranger who is found in the streets after dark without a light, and to look well to the protection of the houses and

[1] Job xxvii. 18.　　　　[2] Canticles i. 6.

shops in their respective districts. The disconsolate and bewildered bride, rashly venturing out of doors at midnight, alone, without a lantern, and with wild cries, is represented as immediately seized and very roughly handled by these keepers, as certainly would be the case now.

> "The keepers that go about the city found me,
>   They smote me, they wounded me ;
>   The keepers of the walls took away my veil
>   from off me." [1]

For several months in the year, dwellers in Palestine leave the hot towns and villages, and reside in tents, or small houses, in adjacent cool and elevated districts, thus taking change of air without quitting their ordinary avocations. This appears to have been the custom from time immemorial. Not only on these occasions, but also in travelling, when the tents are pitched in the neighbourhood of any inhabited place, it is usual to apply at once to the governor, or headman of the district, for a keeper to watch over the encampment

---

[1] Canticles v. 7. The word in this instance rendered "keeper," שֹׁמֵר, shoamair, from שָׁמַר, shamar, "to keep watch," or "to guard" (see Jeremiah iv. 17, &c.), is the word usually employed to denote this office. The only exception to this rule is when vineyard cultivation is in question. In this case the words used seem invariably נֹצֵר, noatzair, from נָצַר, natzar, "to keep," or "watch" (Isaiah xxvii. 3 ; Jeremiah iv. 16; Job xxvii. 18), and the very similar cognate form נֹטֵר, noatair, from נָטַר, natar, with the same meaning (Canticles i. 6 ; viii. 11, 12).

by night. The keepers commonly employed in Jerusalem are tall, white-robed, jet-black Nubians, who
are armed with clubs — men of great strength
and dreaded fierceness, yet, notwithstanding, very
loyal and faithful to their employers. I have
myself constantly hired keepers to watch over my
encampment, and can testify to the stern reality of
their labours, when I have suffered, as in a certain
notable instance while in tents near Jerusalem,
from the nocturnal assaults of robbers, one of whom
was secured after a sanguinary struggle. The story
of this occurrence so well illustrates those features
of Palestine life which have from the earliest times
given rise to the office of a keeper, that I cannot
do better than briefly recount it here.

During the hot summer of 1871, while many of
the residents at Jerusalem, according to the custom
I have described, were encamped outside the city
walls, almost nightly robberies took place. Men
were constantly prowling about the tents after dark,
and, as appeals to the authorities produced no
result, very great uneasiness prevailed. The camp
of our mission party was pitched at this time half a
mile west of the city, on the Jaffa road, in a large
enclosure, called from its high and healthy situation
the Sanatorium. In the centre of this enclosure
stood a substantial stone-built house, which served
as the sleeping quarters of the more delicate, while

seventeen tents were grouped before it, forming
a picturesque encampment. We rose at sunrise
and rode into Jerusalem to engage in the labours
of the day, and at sunset we returned to partake of our evening meal, enjoy the cool air, and
retire early to sound and refreshing rest under our
canvas roofs. But the quiet and peace of this
pleasant and healthful life was soon to be broken.
One night a lady of our party, who was sleeping in
a tent alone, was awakened by a movement at her
head, and saw a man, who was making off with a
box, disappear through the door. She was at first
afraid to cry out, and he easily escaped before the
alarm was given. Emboldened by their predatory
success, the robbers attempted to enter three tents
the next night. From that time we ceased to rely
upon our *Muslim* keeper—a man of the adjoining
village of *Lifta*, chosen, as was usual, for his own
somewhat desperate character, as on the whole the
fittest for such a post—and commenced to watch
ourselves. To apply to the hopelessly weak and
corrupt local government was found worse than use-
less. I had already learned, by painful experience,
that Palestine criminals could safely laugh at and
defy the authorities while free, and no less safely
bribe them with their spoils when caught. In
Syria, circumstanced as we were, we could have
little other protection, under God, than that which

we could afford ourselves. Accordingly a great part of the night I kept guard over the camp in turn with others. No more attempts followed for a while, and we began to relax the strictness of our watch.

One night about this time, feeling thoroughly dissatisfied with our keeper Mustafa, who had lately obtained the help of his brother, I called him up, and threatened him severely with the consequences which would follow if we suffered any loss or injury through his neglect. He was thoroughly aroused by the words, which plainly impeached his diligence, courage, and honesty, and, when we retired to rest in our tents, Mustafa and his brother repaired to mount guard, and probably for the first time to keep a faithful watch. At half-past two o'clock we were roused from our beds by a noise, and hastily dressing, I ran out, to find that our keeper's brother had seen a man stealing to one of the servants' tents, but, in the pursuit which followed, he had succeeded in making good his escape. Some time passed in searching the grounds, and we again sought rest in our tents. Hardly, however, had I laid down, before terribly loud but distant cries reached my ears, which more resembled the yells of wild beasts than the shouts of men. I leaped from my camp bed, seized the first weapon which came to hand, which chanced to be an oak club, and, half naked, ran for the spot whence the noise proceeded. I called to others as I started, and a youth armed with a gun followed me. I had to climb two *jĕdars*— walls of loosed piled-up stones—and in perfect darkness to make my way over rough rock boulders, and through formidable thistles and nettles. The yells, however, guided me to the spot, and in another moment I had thrown myself upon three struggling men, to find to my inexpressible relief that Mustafa and his brother were mastering a gigantic fellow, who succumbed on my coming up without further resistance, and to be sprinkled with the blood that had been flowing from their wounds. The youth who had followed me soon reached the scene, and our arrival proved most timely; for three of our prisoner's comrades, who had returned to his aid, now took to flight.

We brought him into our camp, and, having bound his feet in the irons used to fetter our asses, attended to a severe sword-wound on his head. I had rarely seen a more powerful man. He was considerably over six feet, well made in proportion, and the savage glance of his sullen eyes, as he lay bound and cowering amongst us, I shall not soon forget. We then proceeded to the spot where he had first been sighted, and discovered a parcel containing money and clothes, which were afterwards identified as those which he had stolen from a German encampment in an earlier part of the night, and a stonemason's hammer with which he was armed. We also found his turban, which contained between the *tarboosh*, or red cloth cap, and the inner close-fitting skull-cap of white cotton, called *arakiyeh* (the *fellahheen* constantly use them in this way as a kind of pocket-book), a number of letters giving us his name, residence, and occupation. From these he was at once recognised as a man of position and property in a neighbouring village, *Ain Karim*, a long-suspected and desperate character.

Great was our thankfulness at such a merciful providence, and still more so when we learnt how specially it had been exercised. Mustafa, it seems, armed with his sword, had stolen out alone in the direction in which the robber had first come. There, at some distance beyond the wall of our encampment, hidden by a rock, he had watched this man stealthily returning to secure the already stolen booty, which he had dropped when surprised at the first alarm, and which we afterwards found. Upon our keeper showing himself, the man caught sight of him, and said in a low voice, Are you So-and-so? naming one of his companions. Mustafa's answer was an attempt to seize him, when the man turned to fly, but in running fell over a low embankment

in the dark, and was thus caught. A deadly con-
flict now ensued, in which Mustafa lost his sword,
and, notwithstanding his great strength, and the
advantage he had gained, was completely over-
powered. At this moment one of the man's accom-
plices came up, and seizing Mustafa's sword, struck
at the combatant above, whom he mistook in the
darkness for our keeper, and thus inflicted a severe
wound upon the back of his comrade's head. This,
with the arrival of Mustafa's brother, followed by
myself, decided the struggle.

Early next morning a summary trial of the prisoner took place in our camp, the judge and the
officers of the court, together with the representatives
of our English consulate, coming out to the Sanatorium for the purpose. The man raised a clever
defence, but it availed him nothing. When upon
cross-examination he refused to admit that he was
guilty, the officers standing by with brutal violence
struck him on the face with the palms of their
hands, and otherwise cruelly ill-treated him. It
was a painful scene, such as generally occurs at a
criminal trial in Palestine. I witnessed it on that
occasion for the first time. As I looked on indig-
nantly, I realised with awful vividness the depth
of degradation and suffering to which our Saviour
stooped, when He submitted to be treated as a male-

factor of the lowest class in just this way![1] The trial resulted in a sentence to a long term of imprisonment. There was much general rejoicing at the capture of one of those dangerous felons, whom the police are powerless to arrest, and no more tents were molested that year in the neighbourhood.

It is very difficult to find keepers for this work who can be thoroughly trusted. Most native Syrians are afraid to encounter these robbers, who form a desperate class, while many will conspire to plunder the very tents they are hired to guard. Another great practical difficulty is to find a keeper who will *remain awake during the whole night*. The weariness of those who keep a faithful watch, and their longing for day during the tedious lonely hours of darkness, is alluded to in a graphic and beautiful figure of the Psalmist—

" My soul [waiteth] for the Lord

---

[1] Matthew xxvi. 67; xxvii. 30; Mark xiv. 65; Luke xxii. 63–65; John xviii. 22. The Apostle Paul, when tried before the court of the Sanhedrim, was treated in the same manner. When he began to speak in his own defence, Ananias, the High-priest, who was the head of the court, "commanded those that stood by him to smite him on the mouth" (Acts xxiii. 2); but this holy man was not so meek and patient as his Master under similar provocation.

More than keepers for the morning,
[More than] keepers for the morning."[1]

The usual method adopted to secure due vigilance is to require the man to call out loudly, or to blow a whistle, every quarter of an hour. This not only serves to frighten away robbers, but also to assure his wakeful employer that he is diligently on duty. Even when acting as keepers of vineyard or other produce, they cry out loudly at intervals to let it be known that the place is watched. There seems a plain reference to such a practice in the prophet Jeremiah, where down-trodden Jerusalem and Judea are represented as held against their own excluded and rightful possessors as by watchful keepers.

"Behold, cry aloud concerning Jerusalem :
Keepers (*noatzair*) come from a far country,
And *utter their voice* against the cities of Judah.
Like keepers (*shoamair*) of a field are they against
her round about ;
Because she hath been rebellious against me,
saith Jehovah."[2]

Yet, notwithstanding all precautions, as soon as sleep falls on the tired camp, it is too often the case that the hireling keeper lies down on the ground,

[1] Psalm cxxx. 6.   [2] Jeremiah iv. 16, 17.

wraps around him his thick 'abaiyeh, or cloak, and, careless of his charge, or overcome with weariness, yields himself up to his drowsy propensities.

Viewed in the light of these facts, how full of condescension and cheer is the assurance of God's never-ceasing care—

> " He who keepeth thee will not slumber.
> Behold, he who keepeth Israel
> Doth not slumber or sleep.
> Jehovah is thy keeper ! "[1]

While the services of the keeper constitute at all times a marked feature of life in Palestine, they are perhaps more needed when travelling through the country than at any other time. Then, when the moving camp is nightly pitched in strange fields, it becomes absolutely necessary to apply to the nearest authorities for a nocturnal guardian, before one càn safely lie down to rest. Now this Psalm cxxi. being one of " the Songs of Degrees,"

---

[1] Psalm cxxi. 3–5. See also Psalm cxvi. 6—

> "Jehovah is the keeper (shoamair) of the simple,"

and Psalm cxlvi. 9—

> "Jehovah is the keeper (shoamair) of strangers."

In Ecclesiastes v. 8, God's watchful care and supreme providence is described by the same term shoamair, and the same bold and beautiful figure is probably intended. "If thou seest the oppression of the poor, and violent perverting of judgment and justice in the city [or province], marvel not at the matter, for a higher than the high is keeper."

was probably composed to be sung on the way to Jerusalem, as a pilgrim hymn, when the Israelites were coming up annually to keep the three great feasts. As a journeying Psalm, it would therefore have peculiar significance in its allusion to the keeper by night.

CHAPTER IX.

CRUSHED STRAW.

"For in this mountain shall the hand of Jehovah rest ;
And Moab shall be trodden down under him,
Even as crushed straw is trodden down in Madmenah."
—ISAIAH xxv. 10.

ONE of the most peculiar and prominent features of agriculture in the Holy Land is the primitive mode of threshing, or treading down, straw, by which it is crushed to atoms and converted into fodder. Camels, laden with two huge sacks, may constantly be seen carrying the straw when so crushed into the towns where, under the Arabic name of *teben*,[1] it is a regular article of commerce. It forms by far the larger part of the food of horse, mule, ass, ox, camel, and dromedary,—that is, of all the beasts of burden. Indeed the provender of horse, mule, and ass consists only of about one part of barley, mixed with two or three parts of this broken straw, with the exception of fresh barley and other grasses, called *hhasheesh*, during the short six weeks in March and April when they can be

[1] The e in *teben* is sounded short, something like Y.

freely procured. Hay is unknown—straw, in the
form before-mentioned, entirely taking its place.
This seems always to have been the same; for we
read that Solomon's officers provided his stables
with the very food that the Sultan's officers would
procure now: "barley and crushed straw (*teven*) for
the horses."[1] Twice we read in Isaiah that the food
of the ox was *teven*.[2]

Teben, I have said, is the technical Arabic term
for crushed or trodden straw, and this surely must
be the meaning of the very same Hebrew word
teven[3] in all the passages where it occurs in the
Old Testament. The similarity of the Arabic *teben*
and the Hebrew *teven* does not appear to the
English reader as close as it really is. One character in Hebrew, ב, stands for both *b* and *v*, and the
harder consonant is distinguished from the softer
merely by a point or dot in the centre of the letter.
As these points or dots, in common with most of
the kindred vowel marks, are not found in the most
ancient Hebrew manuscripts, or in those of the
Syriac and other cognate languages, or in any of the
ancient monumental inscriptions, it is impossible for
an Oriental scholar to suppose for a moment that
they were originally a part of the inspired text.
While they are no doubt very correct in the main,

---

[1] 1 Kings iv. 28.   [2] Isaiah xi. 7 ; lxv. 25.
[3] תֶּבֶן The e in this word is short like the Arabic.

some manifest and serious errors must be laid to their charge, several of which are noted in this work. There is every probability that the Hebrew word for "crushed straw" was pronounced precisely the same as its Arabic equivalent.

Fortunately our translators have uniformly rendered this word, in all but two passages, by the same English expression. The places, therefore, where *teven* occurs in Hebrew may be readily recognised by the English reader without any reference to the original, for they are in each instance those where the word "straw" is found in our version. In all these places let "crushed or broken straw"— *i.e.,* straw in a very similar state to our chopped hay—be understood as the exact meaning of the Hebrew. Two passages only occur where it is differently translated, but both refer to the same thing. Jeremiah, challenging the false prophets, and bidding the people compare their lying dreams with the true Divine communications, cries—

"What [hath] the crushed straw (*teven*) [to do] with
the wheat? saith Jehovah."[1]

Twenty camel-loads of *teben* are scarcely worth one camel-load of wheat, and though for a brief season they appear mingled together in the heap of the

[1] Jeremiah xxiii. 28. It is "chaff" here in our version, which, it is true, forms a small part of all good *teben*.

threshing-floor, the time is sure to come when they will be clearly distinguished and finally separated. Job says of the wicked—

"They are as crushed straw *(teben)* before the wind,"[1]

a far stronger figure of weakness and instability than "stubble," by which the word is misrendered in our version.

There is a special word in Hebrew for straw in its natural state, *kash*,[2] from *kashash* to gather, which, answering exactly to the same word in Arabic, is sometimes straw with the ear attached, just as it is gathered by the reapers, and sometimes stubble. In the Authorised Version it may be known by its being translated in every case "stubble." What could be plainer as a reference to straw in its natural condition, than the following comparison used of the strength of leviathan—

"A club is counted [by him] as a straw *(kash)*,[3]

where a heavy cudgel is compared to a puny blade of grain in the estimation of the monstrous and invulnerable crocodile.

Keeping this distinction in mind, we shall understand the great difficulty in which the children of

---

[1] Job xxi. 18. The same force is given to another comparison in this book. Speaking of leviathan, the crocodile, it is said in Job xli. 27—

"He esteemeth iron as crushed straw *(teven)*."

[2] קַשׁ   [3] Job xli. 29.

P

Israel were placed by Pharaoh's tyrannical edict, when they had to gather straw in its natural state *kash*, instead of being supplied with ready-made *teven*, or crushed straw. For Pharaoh commanded "the taskmasters of the people and their officers, saying: Ye shall no more give the people *crushed straw* (*teven*) to make brick as heretofore; let them go and gather *crushed straw* (*teven*) for themselves: and the measure [or number] of the bricks which they did make heretofore ye shall lay upon them; ye shall not diminish ought thereof. . . . So the people were scattered abroad throughout all the land of Egypt to gather *straw* (*kash*) for *the crushed straw* (*teven*)."[1] It was this crushed straw that was required to mix with the clay to make sun-dried bricks, as is still the case in Egypt to the present day.[2] It was now about two months to harvest,

[1] Exodus v. 6, 7, 8, 12.

[2] Gesenius derives תֶּבֶן, *teven*, from בָּנָה, *banah*, "to build," from its early use in brickmaking. This helps materially to identify the *teven* of Scripture with crushed or broken straw, the only kind of straw used for this purpose. Such small particles are required to mix in with the clay to make it bind. Since writing the above, the author has observed Lieutenant Conder's interesting notice of a similar use of crushed straw in the present Palestine brick-fields. "The bricks are made in spring by bringing down water into ditches dug in the clay, where chopped straw is mixed in with the mud; thence the soft mixture is carried in bowls to a row of wooden moulds or frames, each about ten inches long by three inches across; these are laid out on flat ground and are squeezed full, the clay being then left to harden in the sun" (*Tent Work in Palestine*, vol. ii. p. 238).

and they would not only have to hunt for last year's straw in the few places where it still remained, but, when they had collected it, would further have to manufacture it themselves into *teben*. In our version the English reader perceives only half their difficulty. But the officers of the children of Israel would understand that when they had managed to find ordinary straw— a rare commodity at any time in Egypt, and then it was almost a year since the last harvest—they had yet to crush it on the threshing-floors by a long and laborious process. Well might they see "that they were in evil case, after it was said, Ye shall not diminish ought from your bricks of your daily task."[1]

While in the West unbroken straw is most extensively used in many ways, such as thatching, plaiting, packing, and littering stable and farmyard floors, in Palestine it is but little employed. There it is sometimes plaited into baskets and trays, twisted into ropes, and stuffed into pack-saddles. Besides these occasional uses, for which only a small quantity is required, I am not aware of its being commonly put to any other purpose. Corn in Palestine, owing to the heat and drought, is much shorter in the stalk than with us, and the straw is therefore necessarily less valuable, except for use in

[1] Exodus v. 19.

its crushed state as fodder and to mix with clay in brickmaking. For both these requirements it has to undergo a similar preparation, forming, as already remarked, a regular agricultural process, which may be witnessed for months together in the dry season in every part of the country. In describing it a few words are necessary on harvest operations in general.

The uncertainty and consequent anxiety attending the gathering in of harvest in our land is unknown in Syria. The weather during summer has an unvarying constancy. Both at the time of harvest, from the latter end of April to the early part of June, and for three or four months afterwards, no drop of rain falls. Thus there is no need of stacking grain, and threshing and winnowing are performed in the open field under a cloudless sky. The threshing-floor is either a tolerably smooth rocky surface, or a piece of ground carefully laid with a well-beaten compost of clay and cowdung. It is generally placed upon some elevated spot, where it is exposed to the wind. Such is the threshing-floor now in existence on the top of Olivet; and such was that of Araunah, which once stood on the summit of Mount Moriah, afterwards the site of the Temple.[1] Here the grain is brought

---

[1] 2 Chronicles iii. 1. The Arabic name for a threshing-floor, *jurun,* or *jurn,* is virtually the same as the Hebrew גֹּרֶן, *goaren.* May not our

in small sheaves upon the backs of camels and asses. These are placed on the floor in a great heap, called a *sobeh*, from which they are raked down to be laid in thin layers in a circle, having the heap for its centre, with a circumference of ten to fifteen yards. Over the grain thus spread out, oxen ranged in a row are kept constantly walking round. In doing so they perform a double office. First they thresh by treading out the corn, which, as it is detached from the ear, being heavier than the straw, either falls below it or is pressed into the soft mass, and thus escapes being bruised. But another process is going on at the same time. The straw, the lighter part, keeps on the top of the trodden surface, and being of a much softer nature than the grain, is gradually crushed into little pieces by the triturating action of the oxen's hoofs.

There is another mode of threshing, much less common, but which I once witnessed on a floor not far from Jerusalem. In this case the cattle are yoked to a rude sledge, constructed of heavy logs of timber, having its under surface full of small sharp pieces of the hard black basalt stone, called *hajr es*

word corn, used for grain generally, come from this Hebrew word *goaren?* The threshing-floor is thus actually put for its contents in the shape of grain, in Deuteronomy xvi. 13 : "Thou shalt observe the feast of Tabernacles seven days, after thou hast gathered in thy corn (גֹּרֶן, *goaren*) and thy wine."

soda, and sometimes of iron points, firmly let into the wood. The sledge, to which oxen or horses are yoked, is then driven over the loose sheaves by a man who stands upon it, and thus adds to its grinding power the benefit of his own weight, while the process is facilitated by another labourer, who moves the straw about occasionally with a wooden pronged fork. This heavy sledge is doubtless Isaiah's " sharp threshing-sledge having teeth."[1] It is still called *moarej* by the *fellahheen,* which with the invariable softening of the *g* into *j* is the same as the Hebrew word *moarag.*[2] Such "threshing-sledges" Ornan offered to David as fuel for the altar he was about to erect.[3] From their great size it can be seen that they would furnish sufficient wood to consume the sacrifice of two oxen, for which purpose flails, our "threshing instruments," would be wholly inadequate. Sometimes the threshing-sledge, instead of having "teeth" of stone or iron on its under side, is furnished with a number of little wooden rollers, or wheels, bound with iron tires, which turn round as it is drawn along, and serve the same purpose. The classical reader will call to mind that the Roman *tribulum* mentioned by Virgil, and described by Varro in the fifty-second chapter of his first book, was of these two kinds. The latter tells us that the threshing machine with

---

[1] Isaiah xli. 15.   [2] מוֹרַג   [3] 1 Chronicles xxi. 23.

rollers, used specially in a part of Spain, was known as the " Carthaginian waggon." What more likely than that this was brought to the colony of Carthage in the first instance from the shores of Palestine by its Phœnician or Canaanitish founders?

In that interesting passage in Isaiah, where the varied processes of agriculture are set forth as an illustration of the different methods of working which God adopts in His spiritual husbandry amongst men, both these instruments are enumerated as used in moderation to thresh out corn.

> " The *ketzahh* [1] are not threshed with a threshing-
> sledge (*hharootz*),[2]
> Neither is a cart wheel rolled upon the cummin ;
> But *ketzahh* are beaten out with a staff (*matteh*),
> And cummin with a club (*shaivet*).
> Bread [that is, corn] is bruised,
> But he will not ever be threshing it ;
> He driveth the wheels of his cart, and his horses,
> And he bruiseth it not."[3]

---

[1] קֶצַח A kind of sesame, or rape seed, grown for oil, still known by this name in Palestine, and still beaten out in the same way.

[2] חָרוּץ

[3] Isaiah xxviii. 27, 28. Horses are still used in threshing in Asia Minor, though they are seldom so employed in Palestine. Dr. Van Lennep describes this as follows :—" The heaps of sheaves are first spread out evenly upon the floor, in a diameter of fifty or sixty feet. Seven or eight of the horses are then tied to each other by a single rope, so as to stand abreast from the centre to the circumference of the circle. The driver holds the end of the rope with one hand, or fastens it to an upright post in the centre, while with the other he whips the animals to keep them moving abreast in a circle around

The *hharootz*, from the root *hharatz*,[1] the primary
notion of which seems to consist in sharpness, is
the technical name of that form of threshing-sledge
which has sharp teeth on its under side, and "the
wheel of the cart" is the threshing-sledge having
rollers. We have here the origin of our word
tribulation, from the Latin *tribulum*, a threshing-
sledge, and can observe its singularly appropriate
and beautiful meaning. The harsh action of the
heavy-armed sledge as it rubs and drives out the
corn, and crushes and breaks up the heap, fully
illustrates the true action of trial and affliction.
While the chaff and straw are bruised and broken
to atoms, the effect of the *tribulum* on the good
wheat is only to separate it unhurt, purified from
its surroundings—the precious from the vile.
Thus "we must through many tribulations enter
into the kingdom of God"—for sanctified affliction
to the believer is gain, and not loss.[2] It purifies
his nature, but preserves him unhurt for the
heavenly garner.

The work of threshing is more quickly done by

him, as he stands in the middle of the heap. The outside horses
of course have the most travelling to do, and so he frequently
changes their relative position by holding in turn each of the extre-
mities of the rope, so that the horses at the other end of the line
alternately walk at the circumference or at the centre " (*Bible Lands
and Customs*, by H. J. Van Lennep, D.D., vol i. p. 80).

[1] חָרִץ   [2] Acts xiv. 22 .

means of these instruments, but it would appear that their use was always somewhat rare. The process of duly preparing the straw for fodder is better performed by the hoofs of cattle than by any mechanical contrivance. So say the *fellahheen*, who point out that in this simple way not only is it chopped sufficiently fine, but at the same time the broken pieces are properly bruised and softened, and so made more palatable as provender. Where, therefore, labour is cheap, and time, owing to prolonged fine weather and the impossibility of ploughing before the rain, not of much consequence, and cattle-food, consisting chiefly of this crushed straw, a very important matter, the slower process came naturally to be preferred. Hence the verb "to thresh" in Hebrew, *doosh*,[1] is a word which primarily means "to trample down," "to tread under foot."[2]

When the grain is all beaten out, and the wind serves—that is, every day that it blows from the west between noon and sunset, which it does constantly at this season—the heaps, now entirely broken up, are tossed into the air with a winnowing fork. The grain, being heaviest, falls straight down; the *teben*, or crushed straw, being lighter, is carried by the breeze and falls aslant, forming a

---

[1] דּוּשׁ

[2] Job xxxix. 15, "The wild beast *may trample* them;" Daniel vii. 23, "The fourth beast . . . *shall tread it down*."

heap a little farther on; while the chaff, *moatz,*[1] lighter even than the straw, is carried farther still, sometimes forming a third little heap by itself, and sometimes being quite blown away. It will be seen that this adds a further force to the graphic representation of the wicked already noticed—

" They are as crushed straw (*teven*) before the wind,
 And as chaff (*moatz*) that the whirlwind carrieth away ! "[2]

When thus separated from the grain, the crushed straw is again laid by itself on the threshing-floor, and further subjected for a whole day to the trampling of oxen—for its value entirely depends upon its fineness. This second treading-down, or threshing, of crushed straw by itself — a constant practice to be witnessed during summer and autumn in every village of Syria—has not yet, I believe, been brought to the notice of commentators. My attention was first called to it by purchasing on one occasion a very inferior kind of *teben* for the use of my stables in Jerusalem. Having shown a specimen of this provender to a *fellahh,* a neighbouring farmer, he pronounced it only half prepared, and needing the usual second subjection to the feet of oxen. At his proposal some of his own cattle were brought into the city, and for a considerable part of a day were driven round upon

---

[1] מוֹץ   [2] Job xxi. 18.

the *teben*, as it lay spread upon the pavement of my stable-yard. At the close of this "treading-down" it was found to be in excellent condition. The *fellahh* informed me that the Syrian farmers constantly sent such half-prepared *teben* into the towns as soon as the corn was winnowed out, whilst with that reserved for their own use they were in the habit of doing what he had done with mine.

This further process throws light on several passages of Scripture. Take, for instance, that merciful provision of the law, "Thou shalt not muzzle the ox when he treadeth down" (that is, thresheth), which is twice used by the Apostle Paul as an eloquent allegory of the truth "that the labourer is worthy of his hire," and the Christian minister of support from the Church.[1] In our version it is when "he treadeth out *corn*." But this word "corn" is carefully omitted in the original, and has been wrongly inserted by our translators. If the ox is only treading down *teben*, his own proper food, from which the grain has been already removed, he is equally to be allowed to pick up what he needs, as he patiently plods along, or stops at intervals for rest. This Mosaic law is everywhere observed in

---

[1] Deuteronomy xxv. 4; 1 Corinthians ix. 9; 1 Timothy v. 18. The Greek word in these two last verses simply means "threshing," as in the Hebrew.

Palestine by a peasantry who otherwise are very unmerciful in their treatment of dumb animals. The *fellahh* who employs his oxen, and sometimes his asses, in this work of treading, will never muzzle them at such time, and he will tell you, if interrogated on the subject, that it is a great sin to do so.

Again, we read of the destruction brought on the kingdom of Israel in the days of Jehu's idolatrous son by Hazael, king of Syria: "And he (Hazael) left of the people to Jehoahaz only fifty horsemen, and ten chariots, and ten thousand footmen; for the king of Syria had destroyed them, and had made them like the dust in threshing."[1] Here the allusion, probably a proverbial expression, refers only to the crushing up into tiny pieces of the heap of broken straw when laid by itself. Corn is never threshed in this way, for such a treatment would destroy it. The separate heaps of *teben*, however, are purposely subjected to a long and violent treading down—the sole object in their case being to bruise them in every part, and to crush them to atoms. Another similar example is furnished in the passage of Isaiah before referred to—

"Behold, I will make thee into a new sharp threshing-sledge
   having teeth;

---

[1] 2 Kings xiii. 7.

Thou shalt thresh mountains, and beat [them] small,
And shalt make hills as chaff;
Thou shalt fan them, and the wind shall carry them away,
And the whirlwind shall scatter them." [1]

The comparison of mountains and hills to the huge heaps on the threshing-floor is a bold and striking figure, whilst the reference to the wind carrying them away plainly identifies the heaps in question with those consisting entirely of *teben*. The whole process of winnowing in Palestine proceeds, as I have shown, on the principle that the wind is not strong enough in the warm season, except on very rare occasions, to do this in the case of corn. The following quotation from the prophet Micah requires the same explanation—

"Arise and tread down, thou daughter of Zion !
For I will make thine horn iron,
And I will make thy hoofs copper,
And thou shalt beat in pieces many peoples." [2]

Here the picture is that of Zion enabled at last to trample down her proud persecuting foes, even as in threshing a powerful heifer crushes under her feet the heap of broken straw. From all these passages we may draw the conclusion that, according to the general use of types throughout Scripture to signify in each instance the same thing, unless the contrary is expressly stated, *teven*, or crushed straw,

---

[1] Isaiah xli. 15.   [2] Micah iv. 13.

always occurs as a figure of the wicked, the enemies of God and His people.

In the light of this explanation we may now turn to examine the somewhat difficult passage in Isaiah which stands at the head of this chapter. In our version it reads—

> " For in this mountain shall the hand of the Lord res
> And Moab shall be trodden down under him,
> Even as straw is trodden down for the dunghill." [1]

Many have maintained the last words should read, " in the waters of the dungpool." These see in the language of the next verse—

> " And he shall spread forth his hands in the midst of it,
> As a swimmer spreadeth them forth to swim,"

a representation of Moab pressed down into the same pool. But this explanation, together with the rendering of our translation in the preceding verse, turns on a misconception. No dungpool exists in Palestine, much less any treading down of straw in such a place. In the corn lands and pastures no manure requiring carriage is now used, and there is every reason to believe that no such manure was ever thought necessary. Vast caves throughout the mountains of Judah, the home of wild pigeons, are full of guano, while some of smaller size, that serve as winter cattle-sheds, are not much less rich, but all

---

[1] Isaiah xxv. 10.

are left undisturbed, except such as are in the neighbourhood of "watered gardens." The carcases of
horses, mules, asses, and even of huge camels, are left
to rot where they fall on the border of the fields, no
one even so much as covering them with earth.
Few sights in Palestine seem stranger than this to a
Western eye. But for the troops of hyenas, jackals,
and wild dogs that infest the country, and the
immense number of all kinds of huge vultures and
other carrion birds, this neglect would be a fruitful
source of pestilence. In a word, these wonderfully
fertile arable lands never receive any manure that
requires to be carried. Excessively heavy rains
and fierce heat, falling on a soil peculiarly deep and
rich, and constantly crumbling over it the limestone
rock of which the mountains are composed, together
with the fallow of a sabbatic year, seem to have
rendered the land abundantly productive without
any farmyard or artificial dressing. In horticulture,
it is true, manure is freely employed, but principally
dry goat's-dung, and in the north of Syria for melon
and cucumber beds, pigeon-dung, procured from
towers in which these birds are fed and preserved
in vast numbers for this purpose.[1] The sweepings
of stable or cowshed are esteemed of little value.
Swine are still, as anciently, prohibited by ceremonial law. Cowdung is commonly used, by the

[1] Isaiah lx. 8 ; Luke xiii. 8.

poorest of the people, when fashioned into cakes and
dried in the sun, but only as fuel.[1] Manure is never
manufactured or used in a liquid state. The expression, "like dung on the face of the earth," may
allude to that state of the streets and byways in
the villages and towns, which so shocks a traveller
or resident on his first coming to the country.[2]
That for the conduct of which careful sanitary
provision was made under the law while Israel were
encamped in the desert—a very necessary subject
for legislation amongst Oriental nations—now takes
place everywhere without what we should consider
due regard either to decency or cleanliness.[3] As
neither drainage nor cesspools exist in any of the
primitive towns or villages, this usage appears
ancient, though no doubt under a good government
it was not allowed to constitute the nuisance which
it is now. Nothing therefore like the dungpool which
some commentators have imagined has any existence.
In each village the refuse matter is thrown out on
to one large heap, "the dunghill" of Scripture, very
wisely kept dry, and from time to time publicly
burnt, amidst much festive mirth. Hence, with an
intensity of meaning that we are apt to miss, dung
stands in the Bible for that which is utterly vile
and worthless.[4]

[1] Ezekiel iv. 15.   [2] 2 Kings ix. 37 ; Jeremiah xvi. 4.
[3] Deuteronomy xxiii. 12, 13.   [4] Job xx. 7.

But to return to the verse in question. The true translation, which will be found suggested in the margin of the Bible, is as follows :—

> " And Moab shall be trodden down under him,
> Even as crushed straw is trodden down in Madmenah."[1]

This rendering, with reference to what has gone before, will be seen to bring out a powerful and consistent figure, and one in perfect keeping with that of the next verse. There, evidently speaking still of the Lord, it is said—

> " And he shall spread forth his hands in the midst
>   of it (Mount Zion),
> As a swimmer spreadeth [them] forth to swim.
> And he will bring down their pride,
> Together with the plots of their hands."[2]

All swimmers in the East use " hand over hand " swimming, that is, they raise each arm alternately as high as they can, and bring it down upon the water with sounding force. The action, therefore, of stamping to pieces with the feet in the tenth verse is represented in the next as followed by

---

[1] The latter part of the verse adopting the *keri*, which is confirmed by many of Kennicott's best codices, reads : · · · מוֹאָב מַתְבֵּן בְּמוֹ מַדְמֵנָה—*Moav* . . . *mathbain bĕmo Madmainah.* Here the unusual form of *mathbain* for *teven*, and *bĕmo*, the well-known form of the preposition *bĕ* in an elevated style of writing, appear plainly expressions employed in this place to preserve the much-prized alliteration peculiar to the poetry of the prophets.

[2] Isaiah xxv. 11.

Q

repeated blows with the arm, even as a swimmer, lifting each hand in turn above his head, brings it down with all his might upon the surface of the water.

The place mentioned would naturally be the Madmen in Moab itself, for Madmenah is only the feminine form of this name.[1]   There is reason for supposing that the region of Madmen was famous for abundant harvests of grain, and consequently for extensive and well-known threshing-floors.   The *Belka*, a high and extensive tableland, which forms one of the finest corn-producing districts of Syria, lies here.   Moab, it must be remembered, is throughout Scripture a special type of the enemies of the Lord and His people.   In this extended sense we must understand Balaam's prophecy of Christ—

> " And a club (*shaivet*) shall rise out of Israel ;
> And shall smite the corners of Moab." [2]

The twenty-fifth chapter of Isaiah looks beyond a present deliverance to the final overthrow of the last apostate faction by Messiah at His second coming, and the establishment of Israel and the Church in everlasting peace.   Here, as elsewhere, the final struggle is represented as taking place in and around Jerusalem.   The forceful figures of trampling and striking down in the two verses we have been con-

---

[1] Jeremiah xlviii. 2.   [2] Numbers xxiv. 17.

sidering set forth the defeat of the world powers, and the ruin of the finally impenitent " at the revelation of the Lord Jesus from heaven with His powerful angels, in flaming fire, rendering vengeance to them that know not God, and to them that obey not the gospel of our Lord Jesus." [1] Of that time He has Himself declared—

> " I will tread them in mine anger,
> And trample them in my fury." [2]

While His judgments shall pass harmlessly over His own people (the wheat), who will have been first safely gathered into His garner, His enemies shall be broken to atoms like the crushed and trodden straw !

[1] 2 Thessalonians i. 7, 8. [2] Isaiah lxiii. 3.

CHAPTER X.

· *SIFTING.*

"For lo, I will command,
And I will sift the house of Israel among all the
    nations,
As [corn] is sifted in a sieve,
And not a small stone shall fall upon the earth."
                —Amos ix. 9.

CORN in Palestine, after it has undergone the highly
primitive processes of threshing and winnowing, described in the last chapter, comes into the market
in a mixed and unclean condition. Dust and stones
of the open-air threshing-floor, light and damaged
grains of wheat, a small sprinkling of barley, and
seeds of several wild grasses, notably the black
zowan, the bitter and poisonous " tares " of Scripture,
which when first growing cannot be distinguished
from the wheat, mingle largely in the samples
offered for sale in the bazaars. Neither the agri-
culturist nor the merchant cleans the corn, and it is
this fact that has to a great extent discredited the
splendid wheat of Syria in English markets. But

this forms no drawback to the consumer in the Holy Land, who lays in his annual stock of grain after each year's harvest, and, so that there be good wheat and a sufficient proportion of it in that which he purchases, makes but little account of what else it may contain. The fact is that the separation of the refuse from the corn is regularly made from time to time in each household. Among the poor this is made by the husband or wife, and in the case of the well-to-do by their servants, or more generally by those workpeople, male and female, who make this a special branch of labour. Hence arises the distinct process of sifting, which, although it is to be observed going on all the year round in most families throughout the land, forming a very striking and marked feature of Palestine life, I do not remember to have seen anywhere described. It is very vividly impressed on my memory as one of the novel and deeply-interesting sights with which I soon became familiar in our parsonage home on Mount Zion.

The sieve used for this purpose, called *ghurbal*, though shallow, is a very large one—about an Eastern yard, that is, two and a half feet in diameter. The native woman seats herself on the floor, generally in the courtyard of the house, with her feet spread widely apart, and holds the sieve half full of wheat between her two hands. She begins the process, in which great dexterity is displayed, by shaking the

ghurbal from right to left six or seven times, till all
the crushed straw and the chaff that still remains in
the corn comes to the surface, most of which she is
able to gather up and throw away.   Then she commences to hold the sieve in a slanting position, and
for a considerable length of time jerks it up and
down, blowing vigorously across it all the while with
her mouth.   This part of the manipulation, which
is most skilfully performed, has three results.   First,
the dust, earth, barley, and small grains of wheat
fall through the meshes of the sieve on the ground
between her feet.   Next, chiefly by means of the blowing, the remaining *teben* and chaff is either dispersed
or collected in that part of the *ghurbal* which is
farthest from her.   Thirdly, the best of the wheat
goes to the bottom in one heap, while at the same
time the small stones are collected together in a
little pile by themselves, on that part of the sieve
which is nearest to her chest.   She then removes
with her hands the stones, *teben*, and chaff.   After
this she sets the *ghurbal* down, and carefully going
over the corn picks out any impurities which may
yet remain.   The "sifting" is then complete.   The
refuse that has fallen through the sieve in a heap
between her feet is again subjected to a similar operation in a finer *ghurbal*.   The best part of it, consisting of some grains of light wheat mixed with
barley, called *rádáyed*, is generally ground and

A BETHLEHEM WOMAN SIFTING WHEAT.

baked separately, while the remaining mixture, composed of very small grains of wheat, black *zowan*, or tares, and other grass seeds, is used to feed fowls.

Often have I stood to watch this primitive but dexterous process, which, as it is the same in every part of the land, is in all probability that to which Divine allusion is twice made in the Scriptures.[1] It

---

[1] Amos ix. 9 ; Luke xxii. 31. The passage in Isaiah where, in our version, Jehovah is said to threaten to "sift" the nations who are gathered together at Armageddon against restored Israel "with the sieve of vanity," is clearly a misrendering, and appears to have no reference to the sifting which is described above. The verse, Isaiah xxx. 28, is literally—

> "And his breath [is] as an overflowing stream,
> That reacheth even to the neck ;
> To shake the nations with an emptying shaking ;
> And a bridle shall be in the jaws of the peoples, leading them astray."

There are two images of destruction employed here—a deep flood and a mighty wind. Streams which suddenly form in the valleys, when swollen by winter storms, rise with fearful rapidity as high as a man's neck, and sweep away all before them. With such suddenness and overwhelming destruction a burning blast sent by God shall blow upon the assembled hosts with a blowing that shall empty their ranks, as when at winnowing-time the *shirocco* in its boisterous form arises ; and this wild east wind scatters far and wide the heaps of chaff and crushed straw. A deadly wind seems certainly to have been instrumental in the destruction of Sennacherib's host,—a judgment no doubt typical of the destruction of the last of Israel's foes. God says of this Assyrian invader, in Isaiah xxxvii. 7, 29—

> "I will send a *blast upon him* : "
>
> "I will put my ring in thy nose, and my *bridle in thy lips*,
> And I will turn thee back : "

as if in allusion to the threatening in Isaiah xxx. 28. A burning

would be difficult to imagine a bolder or more appropriate figure of searching and ceaseless trial.
Under this representation the prophet Amos foretold
the eighteen centuries of persecution and suffering
which the Jews have so terribly experienced—

> "For lo, I will command,
> And I will sift the house of Israel among all the
>   nations,
> As [corn] is sifted in a sieve,
> And not a small stone shall fall upon the earth." [1]

shirocco wind of more than ordinary vehemence has been known to
prove as fatal as the simoon of the desert, and probably by some
such "blast" upon their exposed camp the 185,000 troops of Sennacherib met their death (Isaiah xxxvii. 36).

[1] Amos ix. 9. The word I have translated "small stone" is the
Hebrew צְרוֹר, *tzĕroar*, the diminutive of צוּר, *tzoor*, a rock or
stone. This is plainly the sense in 2 Samuel xvii. 13, where
Hushai uses the hyperbolical figure of drawing a whole city with
ropes into the adjacent river, "until there be not even a small stone
(*tzĕroar*) found there." It is most probable that the word in its
other sense, as derived from a root which means "stone," should be
"lump" rather than "bundle," in those passages where the latter
rendering now occurs (1 Samuel xxv. 29; Job xiv. 17; Canticles
i. 13). Lieutenant Conder, R.E., while working on the survey of
Palestine, made an interesting discovery of this word which he found
unknown to educated Arabic-speaking townspeople, but used still
by the *fellahheen* with its old technical meaning. The following
has appeared amongst Notes from the Memoir of the Map :—*Sŭrâr*.
A good instance of the peculiarities of the peasant language is furnished by this word. A native of Beyrout called on me, and I
asked him if he knew what the word meant. Though an educated
man, he could not tell ; but Mr. Bergheim, who lives amongst the
peasantry, informs me that it means "pebbles." Thus the word,
unknown to the townsmen, but retained amongst the peasantry
is the Hebrew *tzĕroar*, "a pebble."

The "tribes of the wandering foot and weary breast" have been dispersed into every land, and yet have failed to find anywhere a place of quiet habitation. Driven hither and thither, now the victims of avaricious kings and nobles, and now the sport of a cruel and ignorant populace, they have been like wheat tossed in a sieve. Theirs has been a history of unrest without a parallel in the life of any other people. Truly they have been sifted "among all the nations—

'As [corn] is sifted in a sieve.'"

And yet He who gave the "command" for this has done so not with a view to their destruction, but to their purification. Most appropriately has He likened the painful discipline to which He has subjected them to "sifting," for His purpose in it throughout has been to prepare them to take their place amongst the good wheat. From time to time "the good seed," "the children of the kingdom," "the remnant according to the election of grace," have been gathered out of them, and added to the Church of the Firstborn. But even the hard-hearted, stony-ground members of this marvellously preserved people, though worthless as the pebbles amongst the grain, have not been allowed to perish, for so have been fulfilled the words—

"And not a small stone shall fall upon the earth."

Through all, the Hebrew race has remained intact, a standing miracle of Divine providence in the sight of the whole world. What other people have survived the loss of their national polity, their land, their liberty, and the favour and respect of all their fellow-men, among whom they have been a "byword, a hissing, and a reproach"? Yet this has been the case with the sifted seed of Abraham, and in their miraculous preservation they stand as a lonely but living monument of hoary antiquity to attest the truth of the Bible.

The same figure is employed with equal force in our Lord's warning words to Peter. "Simon, Simon," the Master declared, "behold, Satan asked to have you, that he might sift you as wheat."[1] The bold, loving, and impetuous disciple, at the moment when he was thus addressed, had nerved himself for an act of heroism, and in vain self-confidence thought himself fully equal to its performance. In answer to this solemn warning, he replied earnestly, "Lord, with thee I am ready to go both to prison and to death." Brave indeed he was at the arrest in the garden of Gethsemane, and, had this been the climax, as he sprung forth, sword in hand, to defend his Lord, he would have been in no danger of denying Him.[2] But Peter little knew the subtlety of that arch-foe,

[1] Luke xxii. 31.   [2] John xviii. 10.

whom more than the cunning of Jewish priests, or the violence of Roman soldiers, he had cause to fear. A night of terrible confusion and anxiety followed, a night of slow anguish and great perplexity, during which our Blessed Lord was hurried from one hostile tribunal to another, and sudden surprises followed in swift succession. Introduced after dark into the high priest's palace, the humble fisherman of Galilee found himself in very new and untried circumstances. Characters naturally sanguine, bold, and impetuous, like that of Peter, are almost always deficient in the quality of patient endurance, which, humanly speaking, alone could have enabled him to bear up against the long and unexpected terrors and humiliations of that weary night. Satan was thus, with fiend-like malice, "sifting" the disciple of Christ. He was keeping him constantly tossed about, as skilfully and diligently as an experienced sifter keeps the contents of a sieve of wheat continually moving. He was thus seeking to find out and bring to the surface all that was bad and worthless in the apostle's character, and we know that his hellish exploit succeeded. Well was it for the tried disciple that he was enjoying the inestimable benefit of Jesus' special intercession, that the Lord had prayed for him that his faith might not utterly fail, and that this sad experience might be made the means of his true conversion. Satan's malice was baffled, and Peter went out from the high priest's palace not only a sadder, but a wiser and a better man. Satan's cruel and malicious dealings with Peter were thus overruled by God, to the true end for which all sifting is employed, namely, the purification of that which is subjected to the process. The devil was seeking to bring to light the corruptions of Peter's heart, in order to pour contempt on the truth in the person of one of its most eminent professors, and in order to destroy the apostle himself by driving him to despair through the display of his sinfulness. This is his cunning and wicked design in all the temptations and perplexities with which he is allowed to vex the children of men. But the omnipotent grace of Him who is stronger than the strong is ever bringing good out of evil, and even Satan, in His mighty hand, becomes only a blundering slave to sift the wheat, that is thus, as by a final process, prepared for the Master's use!

CHAPTER XI.

THE SHEPHERD'S CLUB AND STAFF.

"Thy club and thy staff they comfort me."
—PSALM xxiii. 4.

THE Syrian shepherd has two implements of his calling, neither of which is wanting when he is on full duty. If his scanty dress is examined, it may be seen to consist of a *kamise,* or unbleached calico shirt, gathered in round the waist by a strong red leather belt.[1] Hung to this belt, "the leathern

---

[1] Over the *kamise,* in wet or cold weather, and during the night, the shepherd, like all other peasants, wears a thick, warm, sleeveless, sack-like outer garment, made of camel's-hair, invariable as to material, shape, and colour, the latter being dark brown of different shades, with whitish perpendicular stripes. This is the common overcoat of the agricultural labourer and of all the working classes of the country districts. In allusion to the proverbial ease with which this loose simple garment is put on, it is said that Nebuchadnezzar shall "array himself with the land of Egypt," that is, possess himself of its spoils, "as a shepherd putteth on his outer garment (*beged*)" (Jeremiah xliii. 12). When we read that John the Baptist had "his outer garment of camel's-hair, and a leathern girdle," it is the same as saying that he went about dressed not like a well-to-do priest, but like a poor peasant ; and with this agrees the statement that his food was "locust beans and wild honey" (Matthew iii. 4).

girdle " of Scripture,[1] which all workmen or labourers
wear, beside his rude clasp-knife and small leather
pouch, or "scrip," is a formidable weapon of defence,
a stout bludgeon now called in Arabic *naboot*, used
to protect himself and his charge from assailants.
It is generally made of a species of oak that is
to be found in fine park-like groves on the high-
lands of Gilead and Bashan. It is about two feet
long, and often has a large number of heavy iron
nails driven into its rounded head, which render it,
in the hands of an expert, a very deadly arm. Sometimes it is fashioned from a species of willow called
saphsaph, most probably the once-mentioned *tzaph-
tzaphah*,[2] and then it is highly prized. This white
wood is peculiarly light, and at the same time
exceedingly tough and strong. The club is easily
attached to the belt, being furnished with a noose
of cord passed through a hole in the end by which
it is grasped. It may often be seen hanging in this
way from the shepherd's girdle during the daytime,
but at night he carries it in his hand.

The nature of the pastures in Palestine and
throughout the East accounts for this strange
adjunct to a peaceful calling. These are altogether
different from ordinary English grazing grounds.
Grass is never sown or cultivated as in the West.
The rich spontaneous growth of the arable plains

[1] Matthew iii. 4 ; Mark i. 6.   [2] צַפְצָפָה. Ezekiel xvii. 5.

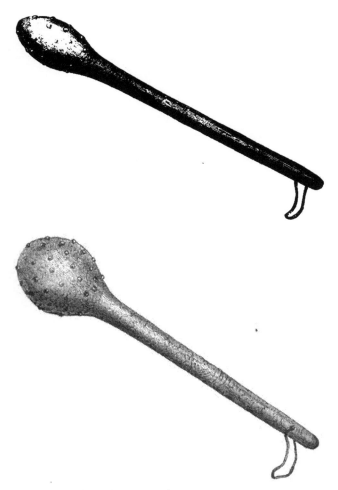

FORMS OF THE SHEPHERD'S SHAIVET OR OAK CLUB.

R.

.

affords good feed, and for a portion of the year
the flocks can be kept on this supply.   For two
months in spring they can be turned out upon those
fields which, being kept for summer crops, are not
sown till late in April.   In autumn they can be
transferred to the stubble-lands from which the
winter crop has been reaped.   But these are not,
strictly speaking, the proper pastures of Palestine.
Such pastures invariably consist of lonely, unfenced,
desert hills, where the sheep are constantly exposed
to a double danger—peril of wild beasts, and peril
of robbers.   It is in obvious allusion to this that
David, comparing himself to a sheep with Jehovah
for his shepherd, says—

"Thou preparest a table before me in the presence of
mine enemies." [1]

These dusty, barren, rocky wildernesses abound
for the most part in caves and hiding-places, which
render them the more insecure, since such of these
spots as can be easily defended are still, as in the
days of Saul, from time to time the resort of bands
of reckless and desperate outlaws.   No dwelling is
to be seen there for a distance of many square miles,
save the low black tents of equally lawless *Bedaween*
Arabs, whose "hand is against every man," that is,
who are a powerful organised confederacy of robbers.
No cultivation is attempted, and the bold shepherd

[1] Psalm xxiii. 5.

alone of all dwellers in town or village frequents
the spot. Such an ordinary sheep-run, the wilderness of Judea, extends for fifteen miles from Jerusalem to Jericho, and, though traversed by an important highway, was, and still is, a very dangerous
place. The outlaws, and the nomad and semi-
nomad Arabs, who wander, like David and his
exile band, over these wild pasture - lands, are
seldom so scrupulous as the followers of the future
king of Israel. When the son of Jesse sent to
Nabal, who fed his sheep at Carmel, the modern
Kurmul, some eight miles south of Hebron, on the
border of this same Judean wilderness, to ask for
a customary *backsheesh,* or present, at shearing time,
he did so on the following grounds : " Thy shepherds
who were with us, we hurt them not, neither was
there aught missing to them, all the days they were
in Carmel." [1] Inmates of some other similar camps
would not have been so forbearing, and the occasional presence of such wanderers in all the principal pastures explains the stalwart shepherd's need
of a weapon of defence.

Wild animals, or "beasts of the field," constitute
perhaps a still greater danger. These to this day
infest all the pastures. The screech of the hyena,
and the yell of the jackal, may even be heard
around the very walls of Jerusalem. Fierce Syrian

[1] I Samuel xxv. 7.

bears and powerful hunting leopards prowl in the less frequented parts. The lion is now never met with west of the Jordan, but was once the terror of the deserts of the land of Israel.[1] Wolves also were common in former times, and are still encountered.[2] These wildernesses, too, are the home of several very venomous reptiles, which in the hot season revel in their crumbled rocks, dust, and heat. Dr. Tristram, speaking of Palestine, says: " The limestone rocks and chalky hills afford the cover and security, both in summer and winter, in which the serpent tribe delights. Under such circumstances they are quickened into a dangerous activity, and their poison becomes very malignant." There is the well-known *Cobra di capello*, and also the *Cerastes* or horned viper. This latter, though it rarely exceeds eighteen inches in length, is a much-dreaded reptile. It has a practice of lying in ambush in pathways, and darting out on any passing animal. It is probably the

> " Adder in the path,
> That biteth the horse's heels,"[3]

to which Dan was likened on account of the acts

[1] Judges xiv. 5 ; 1 Samuel xvii. 34 ; 2 Samuel xxiii. 20 ; 1 Kings xiii. 24 ; 2 Kings xvii. 25.
[2] Isaiah xi. 6 ; Jeremiah v. 6 ; Matthew vii. 15 ; Luke x. 3 ; John x. 12, &c.
[3] Genesis xlix. 17.

of fierceness, cruelty, and treachery which were committed by that tribe. It is so venomous that death ensues in less than half-an-hour after its bite, and it is more vicious than even the cobra, for it will attack unprovoked. The great yellow viper, beautifully marked, and the largest of its tribe in Palestine, is also to be met with, and is especially "dangerous from its size and nocturnal habits." A whitish-yellow scorpion abounds, and the larger and more deadly black species sometimes occurs. Huge birds of prey, with the formidable lammergeyer at their head, still hover above the deserts, out of sight at ordinary times, but ready, with lightning speed, to swoop down on the faint amongst the flock, or even to do desperate battle with the shepherd himself. Hence the obvious need of his being armed; and the principal weapon which he carries, indeed often the only one besides a sling, is the club, or bludgeon, described above.

The guardian of the flock also carries a long shepherd's staff, called *assayah*. Sometimes, though this is rare, it has a curved handle, but in general it is simply a straight strong rod. Its use answers to that of our shepherd's crook, namely, to guide the sheep, to rescue them from danger, to rule the stragglers into order, and at times to chastise the wilful. Thus the Palestine shepherd bears about with him a "club" and a "staff," two entirely different instruments, with distinct and special uses, but both employed in caring for the sheep.

This conveys the full meaning of the royal Psalmist, the once valiant shepherd-boy, when he writes under inspiration—

"Thy club and thy staff they comfort me."[1]

Jehovah's club, that is, His arm of power, will beat down every foe. The good shepherd at the approach of an enemy starts up, drops his staff, or, for greater safety, thrusts it down his back under his *kamise*, and seizing his bludgeon, and securing it to his wrist by the noose, in order that it may not be lost if struck out of his hand, stands prepared to fight to the death with *Bedaween* or bear to protect his charge. "The great shepherd of the sheep, our Lord Jesus Christ," is not less mindful of His flock. When He did battle with the powers of darkness for their salvation, He laid down His precious life. This is the aspect of His work as "the Good Shepherd," so strange to us, but so familiar to an Eastern, on which the Lord dwells in the fourth gospel: "I am the good shepherd: the good shepherd layeth down his life for the sheep. He that is a hireling, and not a shepherd, whose own the sheep are not, beholdeth the wolf coming, and leaveth the sheep, and fleeth, and the

[1] Psalm xxiii. 4.

wolf snatcheth them, and scattereth them. . . . I
lay down my life for the sheep. . . . For this
cause doth the Father love me, because I lay
down my life." [1] Of Him who "was dead and is
alive" we may still say with Nehemiah, "Our God
will fight for us." [2] The day, too, is coming when
Messiah at His second Advent shall "break," or
rather, as it should be, shall "shepherd" all His
enemies and ours with a "club of iron." [3] But the
Lord has also a pastoral staff. With this He guides
us by the way, helps our infirmities, chastens us
when we wander, rescues us from peril, and leads
us back into the "paths of righteousness." O Thou
Good Shepherd! "thy club and thy staff"—Thy
power and goodness, Thy might and mercy, both
alike necessary for my preservation in this wilderness—"they comfort me!"

The club and staff are mentioned as being of
special comfort in a dark, narrow valley.

> " Yea, though I walk through the ravine
>   of the shadow of death,
> I will fear no evil, for thou art with me,
> Thy club and thy staff they comfort me." [4]

---

[1] John x. 11-17.   [2] Nehemiah iv. 20.   [3] Psalm ii. 9.

[4] Psalm xxiii. 4. The word translated "valley" here in our version,
גַּיְא, gay, must be carefully distinguished from עֵמֶק, 'aimek, a broad
plain amongst surrounding mountains, and from בִּקְעָה, bik'ah, like
the same Arabic term, a long deep plain or cleavage between two
parallel lines of mountain ; and also from נַחַל, nahhal, which an-

This scarcely seems to signify the actual dissolu-
tion of the body, although the words may be thus
applied.   It would appear more properly to mean
any season of gloom or imminent danger.   The
figure—a very familiar one to the dweller amid
the fastnesses of Judea, and one which must have
stamped itself with indelible force upon the mind
of David, the whole of whose earlier life was passed

swers to the Arabic *wady*, a long winding valley of whatever shape
which bears a winter watercourse.   Indeed, these various terms,
which are all alike translated " valley " in our version, are used in
the Old Testament with the greatest precision, and are a striking
illustration of the singular power and minute accuracy of the
Hebrew language.   As distinguished from the other words for valley, a *gay* is a ravine, or gorge-like glen.   These deep, narrow glens
abound in the central districts of the country, and form a very picturesque and characteristic feature of Palestine highland scenery.
The Valley of the Son of Hinnom is always called a *gay*—in one
place it is spoken of as "the *gay*" (Jeremiah ii. 23); and the word
used in the New Testament for hell, Gehenna, is only another
form of *Gay* Hinnom.   It came to bear this awful character from its
having been in former times the scene of the hideous fiery worship
of Moloch (2 Kings xxiii. 10; Jeremiah vii. 31, 32); and also from
Tophet being here, the place of filth and refuse, this name being
apparently derived from תֹּפֶת, *thophet*, "an object of loathing"
(Job xvii. 6).   Carcases and other refuse and filthy matter were
brought to this spot, and consumed upon fires kept constantly burning for that purpose.   See Jeremiah xix. 11, 12, 13, and also the
allusion in Isaiah xxx. 33—

> " For long ago hath Tophet been ready,
>   Yea, for the king hath it been prepared ;
>   It is made deep and broad,
>   Its pile is fire and wood in abundance ;
>   The breath of Jehovah, like a stream of brimstone,
>   doth kindle it."

amongst such surroundings—is that of a dark rocky defile, where the path narrows, the cliffs tower overhead, and where the trembling sheep lost upon the mountains is peculiarly exposed to the assaults of enemies. Places of this kind occur repeatedly in the gorges with which the wilderness pastures abound, and the well-known going down from Jerusalem to Jericho affords several striking examples. Huge hyenas, deadly foes to the flock, which hunt at night in small packs, some going before and some waiting behind, easily entrap the sheep in these narrow, dark ravines. David, therefore, when declaring his fearlessness what time he has to go through "the ravine of the shadow of death," is by a bold and beautiful metaphor expressing his confidence in Jehovah's protection in every time of danger. Death certainly is to most men such a season, and moreover Satan often makes a last furious onslaught against the dying believer to distress if he cannot destroy him. But the Good Shepherd is at this supreme moment very near to those who look to Him; and, while they receive comfort from the support of His exceeding great and precious promises as from a staff on which they may safely lean, they receive comfort also from the mace of His mighty power, which drives back the enemies of God and man, and thus guards them in the hour of life's latest peril!

On turning to the original, this distinction between the shepherd's two implements is fully confirmed.   David uses two different words.   The first
is *shaivet*,[1] which, by changes natural to Hebrew,
becomes *shaibt*, or *saibt*, and hence, doubtless, comes
our "sceptre," by which it is frequently rendered
in the English version.   The strong, tapering, oak
club of the shepherd, with its rounded head studded
with powerful iron nails, is the simple origin of the
royal sceptre.   *Shaivet* occurs more than one hundred and thirty times for "tribe," the idea being
derived from the sceptre borne by its chief.   When
used in war, it was made of iron; and clubs, or
maces, of this kind, *always armed with lance-like
projections*, are still to be seen throughout Palestine.
They often appear conspicuously in the public pro-
cessions of the *Derweeshes*, who carry about with
them at those times very ancient weapons.   These
formidable weapons not only have their rounded
heads covered with long sharp spikes, but generally
terminate in a dagger-like point at either end.   Such
were the "three darts," or rather, as it should be
translated, the "three maces " (*shevateem*, the plural
of *shaivet*), which Joab seized, as the first weapons

---

[1] שֵׁבֶט.   There is a closer resemblance than might at first sight
appear between this word *shaivet* and the present Arabic name
naboot, for the consonants are alike, save the substitution of *n*
for *sh*.

that came to hand, and savagely thrust "through the heart of Absalom." [1] At first sight it seems inexplicable to the Hebrew scholar how battle clubs, or maces, could have been used for this purpose, but the construction of the ancient weapons still to be seen in Palestine makes the matter plain. This word "club" is one of the famous titles of Christ. In Balaam's prophecy, the figure of a *shaivet*, or sceptre-club, is applied to Messiah Himself. With reference to the twofold aspect of the Lord's Advent, the son of Beor was inspired to declare—

> "There shall come a star out of Jacob,
> And a club (*shaivet*) shall rise out of Israel,
> And shall smite the corners of Moab,
> And destroy all the children of tumult." [2]

If the Lord Christ is a "star" to Jacob, His own people, cheering and guiding them through the night of affliction, He is also a "club" for chastisement and judgment upon Moab, their enemies and His.

The metaphor of "passing under the club"

[1] 2 Samuel xviii. 14.
[2] Numbers xxiv. 17. Our version reads "children of Sheth." It is possible "Sheth" may be a proper name, in which case it can scarcely mean the third son of Adam, but would have some reference to a well-known Moabite prince or place. It is now by some of the best critics rendered "war" or "tumult," and in this case "the children of Sheth" would mean the "tumultuous, or warlike ones," a very fitting description of the world-powers in these last days.

A DERWEESH'S IRON MACE.

(*shaivet*) occurs in the Old Testament.[1] It is probably, as Jewish writers assert, a process of taking the tithe. The animals were all brought together and placed in pens, and were then passed one by one through a narrow entrance, where the shepherd stood with his club dipped in some colouring matter. As the beasts went by he let the rounded head of the club fall on every tenth, and those thus branded were taken for the tithe. It is in reference to this that God declares of His ancient people in the last days, "I will bring you out from the peoples, and will gather you out of the countries wherein ye are scattered, with a mighty hand and with a stretched-out arm, and with fury poured out. And I will bring you into the wilderness of the peoples, and there will I contend with you face to face. . . . And I will cause you *to pass under the club*, and I will bring you into the bond of the covenant. And I will purge out from among you the rebels and the transgressors against me: I will bring them forth out of the country where they sojourn; and they shall not enter into the land of Israel."[2] Here we have the gathering together of Israel out of the countries where they are now scattered, and at the same time the purging out from amongst them of the rebels,

---

[1] Leviticus xxvii. 32 ; Ezekiel xx. 37.
[2] Ezekiel xx. 34-37.

both strikingly displayed by this figure of gathering together a flock to take out of it a tithe for slaughter. Thus " passing under the club"—the symbol, as we have seen, of Divine power—implies the two purposes for which the Jews are yet to be restored to Palestine whilst still in unbelief. First, for the infliction of a terrible and final judgment. Secondly, for their conversion as a nation, and their complete and glorious restoration to the land of promise.[1]

The other word used by David, *mish'eneth*,[2] uniformly rendered staff in every passage where it occurs, seems to mean a stick, used as a support or stay, a long staff, such as is used to this day by aged men to support their steps, or by a shepherd in tending his flock.

Viewed in this light, the twenty-third Psalm clearly explains an otherwise obscure passage in the prophet Micah. As given in our version it is—

> " Feed thy people with thy rod (*shaivet*),
> The flock of thine heritage." [3]

The word "feed" here, *ra'ah*,[4] is not merely to supply with food, but is a technical expression, " to shepherd"—that is, to do all that is implied

---

[1] See *Palestine Repeopled*, seventh edition, pp. 38–50.
[2] מִשְׁעֶנֶת   [3] Micah vii. 14.
[4] רָעָה. This word is the exact equivalent of the Greek ποιμαίνειν, *poimainein*, " to tend as a shepherd."

in the office and care of a shepherd.   The prophet
is speaking of the return of Israel to their own
land.   To make place for the chosen people, the
heathen must be driven out.   Regarding his nation
as a defenceless flock, thrust away from their rightful pastures, Micah calls upon " the Good Shepherd "
to use on their behalf the mace, or " club of iron,"
shaivet barzel, with which King Messiah is represented in the second Psalm as scattering the
heathen.   The lines should be rendered—

> " Shepherd thy people with thy club,
>   The flock of thine heritage."

The answer of the Lord in the next three verses
plainly implies the nature of that pastoral care for
which the prophet cries—

> " The nations shall see,
>   And shall be ashamed of all their might.
>
> They shall lick dust like a serpent,
> They shall come trembling out of their holes
> Like worms of the earth :
> They shall be afraid of Jehovah our God,
> And shall fear because of thee." [1]

---

[1] Micah vii. 16, 17. Compare with this Zechariah xi. 4–7, which
requires a similar explanation, speaking also, as it does, of the
interposition of God on behalf of His ancient people Israel, who,
like a helpless flock, are at the mercy of foreign oppressors, and
deserted by their own unfaithful shepherds. " Thus saith Jehovah
my God : *shepherd* the flock of slaughter ; whose buyers slay them
and hold themselves not guilty, . . . and their own shepherds spare

s

This figure of the shepherd's club is most important in its bearing upon the representation of Messiah's vengeance on His impenitent enemies given in the second Psalm. In our version it is—

" Thou shalt break them with a rod of iron." [1]

The Septuagint, Syriac, and Vulgate versions translate it—

" Thou shalt *shepherd* them with a club of iron." [2]

This might leave the matter doubtful, if we did not possess an inspired authority. Once, however, in the Revelation, the passage is applied to Christ, and twice to His people, and in each instance the

---

them not. For I will no more spare the inhabitants of the land, saith Jehovah. But lo, I will deliver the men, every one into his neighbour's hand. . . . And I *shepherded* the flock of slaughter, even you the poor of the flock " (Zechariah xi. 4–7). Here, as in Micah vii. 16, 17, we may gather from the whole context that the shepherding evidently applies not to "feeding," but to fighting for, and protecting the flock, which is represented as in danger of slaughter.

[1] Psalm ii. 9. The expression here "rod of iron" is שֵׁבֶט בַּרְזֶל, *shaivel barzel.*

[2] That is, instead of תְּרֹעֵם, *teero'aim*, from רָעַע, *ra'a'*, "to break," they read תִּרְעֵם, *teer'aim*, from רָעָה, *ra'ah*, "to shepherd." It is only a question of the vowel points. The consonants תרעם, tr'm, which in the earliest MSS. we know stood alone, may be read either way. It is a striking instance of those errors which have crept in with the points. Remove these here, and a grave difficulty entirely disappears, for the New Testament and the Septuagint then contain a perfectly truthful and literal rendering of the Hebrew.

inspired Greek quotation has the technical expression " to shepherd," rendered in our version " to rule." [1]   With this Divine quotation, surely there cannot be any doubt as to the right reading, and the figure at once becomes consistent and powerful.

" Thou shalt *shepherd* them with a club of iron,"

that is, treat them as a shepherd deals with those who rob or injure his sheep.

One important part of the office of the under-shepherd, the minister of Christ, is here illustrated. He, like his Master, is not only to feed and nourish the souls committed to his care, but also to be prepared to guard them from their foes at the cost, if needs be, of suffering and loss.   The Apostle Paul, that pattern minister, was thus constantly laying down his life for others.   To "false brethren," he tells the Galatians, he "did not yield submission, even for an hour; that the truth of the gospel might continue with you." [2]   Painful as it must have been, when he thought the Apostle Peter's conduct likely to injure others, he "withstood him to the face, because he was evidently to blame" for

[1] Revelation ii. 27; xii. 5; xix. 15. This application to the believer of Messianic passages which apply in the first instance to Christ, occurring as it does in a number of other instances, sets forth very beautifully the intimate union which exists between the saint and his Saviour.

[2] Galatians ii. 1-5.

his act of dissimulation, in withdrawing himself from the Gentiles through fear of certain Jews who had come from Jerusalem.[1] This consideration, too, adds much to the deep meaning of Jesus' tender restoration of His penitent disciple, which is literally, " Simon, son of Jonas, lovest thou me ? . . . *shepherd* my sheep."[2] The significance of these pathetic words is heightened by the fact that the Lord at once proceeded to prophesy that Peter, who fell through fear, would indeed be dauntless and faithful in the pastoral office, and glorify God by the cruel death of crucifixion, rather than betray his charge.[3]

The same idea seems to have been in the mind of Paul when addressing for the last time the elders of the Ephesian Church. " Take heed unto yourselves," is his warning cry, " and to all the flock, in which the Holy Spirit hath made you overseers, *to shepherd* the Church of God, which he purchased with his own blood. I know that after my departing grievous wolves will enter in among you, not sparing the flock; and from among your own selves will men arise, speaking perverse things, to draw

[1] Galatians ii. 11-14.
[2] John xxi. 16. The words in verses 15, 17, are respectively, "feed my lambs," "feed my sheep," a technical term for supplying with food being used in these passages.
[3] John xxi. 18, 19.

away the disciples after them."[1]   Here the "shepherding" mainly refers to defending the flock courageously against their spiritual foes.   Hence the allusion to the blood of God having been shed in their behalf, and to the coming in of false teachers, terrible as wolves, though outwardly clad in sheep's clothing, who are to be faithfully resisted.

We are specially warned that in the last days "evil men and impostors will wax worse and worse, deceiving and being deceived."[2]   No wonder that it is said of such a time, "All that desire to live godly in Christ Jesus will suffer persecution."[3]   We need pastors now of David's spirit.   "Thy servant," he tells us, "kept his father's sheep ; and there came a lion and a bear, and took a lamb out of the flock ; and I went out after him, and smote him, and delivered it out of his mouth ; and he arose against me, but I caught his beard, and smote him and slew him."[4]   Such "shepherding" the flock of God requires in our day !   We want men "valiant for the truth," who are not afraid or ashamed of being true Protestants, however unfashionable, ignorant, or uncharitable the spirit of the age may deem them.   We want ministers who, though it involve ignominy and loss, will "contend earnestly

[1] Acts xx. 28–30.   [2] 2 Timothy iii. 13.   [3] 2 Timothy iii. 12.
[4] 1 Samuel xvii. 34, 35.   Probably David's shepherd's club played an important part in smiting these wild beasts.

for the faith once delivered to the saints." We
want bishops and presbyters who are not ashamed or
unmindful of their consecration and ordination vows;
that, the Lord being their helper, they are " ready,
with all faithful diligence, *to banish and drive away
all erroneous and strange doctrines contrary to God's
Word; and both privately and openly to call upon and
encourage others to the same."* In these last days,
error is abroad in countless subtle and dangerous
forms, and Satan, in the disguise of an angel of
light, is spreading new traps for the unwary—
snares sacerdotal, infidel, and materialistic. The
enemies of truth are swiftly gathering, and apparently preparing, as they have never done before,
to unite their forces for the final struggle. At such
a time it surely behoves the faithful pastor to culti-
vate a suffering, self-denying, unworldly spirit, and
do battle courageously on behalf of the flock over
which the Holy Spirit has made him overseer.

CHAPTER XII.

MOUNT ZION.

"They that trust in Jehovah are as Mount Zion,
Which shall not be moved : it abideth for ever.
The mountains are round about Jerusalem ;
And Jehovah is round about His people,
Henceforth, even for evermore."

—PSALM CXXV. 1, 2.

COMPARISONS, or similes, are sometimes used, not only to place a subject in a clearer light, which may be done by commonplace illustrations, but also to amplify and ennoble it. In this case sublime and splendid imagery must be summoned to serve. Perhaps one of the finest examples of this kind of lofty comparison is to be found in the illustration of the privileges of believers, drawn from the immutable strength and danger-defying situation of Mount Zion. It occurs in one of the Songs of Degrees. It is most probable that these "Songs of Ascendings," or "goings up," were sung in chorus by the Hebrew caravans to cheer their yearly journeys to the City of the Great King. May we not well suppose that the eager pilgrim band burst into the 121st Psalm, the second of these songs, as they first caught sight of the heights of Jerusalem, singing—

"I will lift up mine eyes unto the mountains ;
From whence shall my help come."?[1]

Then it would seem that, halting near the gates to form the procession to the sanctuary, they pealed forth the hymn—

"I was glad when they said unto me,
Let us go to the house of Jehovah.
Our feet shall stand
Within thy gates, O Jerusalem !"[2]

And at length arrived, as it would appear, within the Temple area, and looking forth on the sacred, never-to-be-forgotten scene, full of holy joy, they celebrated their mercies and privileges in the following words :—

"They that trust in Jehovah are as Mount Zion,
Which shall not be moved : it abideth for ever.
The mountains are round about Jerusalem ;
And Jehovah is round about His people,
Henceforth, even for evermore."[3]

Many who repeat these soul-stirring Hebrew verses form but a faint conception of their full force. But to those who are familiar with the

---

[1] Psalm cxxi. 1.   [2] Psalm cxxii. 1, 2.
[3] Psalm cxxv. 1, 2.

natural features of the district they possess peculiar
power and beauty.   Mount Zion sometimes stands
for the one hill on the south-western quarter of
Jerusalem, now partly within and partly without
the walls, which in ancient times, however, entirely
encircled its summit; and sometimes for the whole
site of the city, consisting of the seven hills on
which it was situated, namely, Mount Zion, Mount
Acra, Mount Ophel, Mount Moriah, Mount Gareb,
and Mount Goath.[1] In this latter sense, Mount Zion,
as the largest, most anciently inhabited, and most
important part of Jerusalem, stands, by a figure of
speech, for the whole of the triple-walled metropolis of Palestine.   Whether we confine it to the
single mountain in question, or regard it as spoken
of all the seven hills enclosed by the three walls
of the ancient city, Mount Zion would convey
to the mind of an Israelite a very grand representation.   The mountains of Judah in this central
part of the chain, where they rise to the height
of over 2500 feet above the level of the sea,
are composed on the surface, and to a great
depth below, of tertiary limestone of four different
kinds.   There is a nummulitic limestone which
has bands of flint and fossils, called in Arabic
Kacooley; a beautifully white limestone which goes

---

[1] In proof of this statement the reader is referred to the seventh
edition of the author's *Palestine Repeopled,* Appendix D.

by the name of *Malakey*, much used for ornamental
stone work; an exceedingly hard silicious chalk,
also with bands of flints called *Mizzey;* and lastly,
a pink and white strata of indurated chalk, also
exceedingly hard, and taking a fine polish, known
as the "*Santa Croce*" marble. The *Kacooley* and
Malakey rocks are comparatively soft when first
quarried at any depth below the ground, but the
Malakey, wherever it rises to the surface or is
exposed to the air, gradually and constantly hardens,
which renders it a very valuable stone for building
purposes, as I know from actual experience of its
use. The *Malakey*, however, in the hills which
form the site of the Holy City, generally under-
lies the marble - like *Mizzey*, or silicious indurated
chalk, which exceedingly hard stone forms most of
the surface rock. In consequence of this feature,
where the *Malakey* crops up near the ground, large
tombs and *beers*, or underground cisterns, have been
excavated in that softer stratum of rock, while the
Mizzey has been left to form the natural roof. The
huge rock-cut cisterns in the present Haram area,
the site of the courts of the Temple, some of
which are forty feet deep, afford a striking example
of such excavations. The *Malakey* stratum has a
depth of forty feet, and the *Mizzey* of seventy-one
feet, in the immediate neighbourhood of the city.
Owing to the great depth to which the hard *Mizzey*

rock descends, all attempts to sink the shaft of an artesian well near Jerusalem have hitherto been abandoned. I have said the *Mizzey* stone prevails upon the surface both in and around the city. The best evidence of this is offered by the fact, that in almost every instance when a man purchases a small plot of land, he finds enough of this stone to build, not only a house and enclosure wall founded upon their own native rock, but also the accompanying *beer*. I have had occasion to excavate much of the *Mizzey* upon my own grounds on Mount Gareb,. and have good reason to know how exceedingly hard, difficult of clearage, and durable it is. Hence it was perfectly natural that Mount Zion should have been pre-eminently regarded from the earliest times as "the level or tableland rock,"[1] the natural, immovable, stone stronghold of Canaan's "everlasting hills."

In a glance at the spot given us in the days of

---

[1] Jeremiah xxi. 13, צוּר הַמִּישֹׁר, *tzoor pameeshoar*, "rock of the *meeshoar*," a Hebrew idiom for "the *meeshoar* rock." This word *meeshoar* means "level down," or "tableland." It is applied specially as a technical and local name to the smooth upland downs of Moab (Deuteronomy iii. 10; Joshua xiii. 17, xx. 8; Jeremiah xlviii. 8, 21). Hence, from the idea of a smooth, plain, lofty place, *meeshoar* came to have the secondary metaphorical sense of "equity," or "justice" (Psalm xlv. 6, lxvii. 4; Isaiah xi. 4; Malachi ii. 6). No doubt, in allusion to this meaning of the word, as well as to its being a level surface on the summit of hills, Jerusalem was proudly called by its inhabitants "the *meeshoar* rock."

David, we learn that it was regarded from time immemorial as a place of such strength, owing to its steep, precipitous, rocky sides, as to be held impregnable,—the Gibraltar of Palestine fortresses. Josephus gives a detailed account of the magnificent natural position of the walls, towers, and fortifications of the city of Herod at this point. His descriptions, which it has been so much the fashion in modern times to decry as enthusiastic and exaggerated, have throughout the work of the Palestine Exploration Fund been for the most part minutely confirmed.[1] This Jewish writer, who was engaged in a leading capacity in the siege of Jerusalem under Titus, tells us that the first of the three enclosure walls ran round the summit of Mount Zion, that it was defended by sixty towers; and speaking of the three named Hippicus, Phasælus, and Mariamne, he describes them as the wonder of all beholders on account of their great height, massive structure, and commanding position. Titus, who destroyed all else, left these as trophies of his splendid victory, to show the exceeding vastness and strength of the fortifications which had been reduced by the might

[1] The principal exception to this rule occurs in the case of his description of the town of Cæsarea. If the ruins now supposed to represent this once important place are on the true site—and it appears to me that this has been by no means indisputably proved —they appear to contradict the magnificence which Josephus recounts.

of Rome. Josephus speaks of them as "for largeness, beauty, and strength, beyond all that were in
the habitable earth." [1] "The largeness also of the
stones," he says, "was wonderful, for they were not
made of common small stones, nor of such large
ones only as men could carry, but they were of
white marble cut out of the rock (probably *Malakey*);
each stone was twenty cubits in length (at least
about twenty-seven feet), and ten in breadth, and
five in depth. They were so exactly united to one
another, that each tower looked like one entire
rock of stone, so growing naturally, and afterwards
cut by the hands of the artificers into present shape
and corners; so little, or not at all, did their joints
or connection appear." [2] Quite recently, in the winter of 1874, Mr. Henry Maudslay, an English civil
engineer, while making improvements in the school
of the Anglican Bishop at Jerusalem on the south-
west brow of Mount Zion, where it overlooks the
pool now called the *Birket es Sultan*, was so fortu-
nate as to fully explore and lay bare the ancient
lie of the rock. Nothing could be grander than the
huge natural fastness, which he was able to follow
and display. The limestone crag proved to have
been scarped, that is, cut smooth and straight as
a wall, with infinite labour perpendicularly to

[1] Josephus' *Wars of the Jews*, book v. chap. iv. sec. 3.
[2] Josephus' *Wars of the Jews*, book v. chap. iv. sec. 4.

the average height of thirty feet throughout the hundred and thirty yards explored on this occasion. The foundation of a mighty tower, a projecting scarp forty-five feet square, was discovered under the school-house, standing itself on a broad ledge of rock, below which another deep scarp appeared to exist. In one place thirty-six steps were laid bare, cut in the face of the scarp ascending the base of a second smaller tower. The bases of three towers in all were examined, and a system of no less than eighteen *beers*, or cisterns, cut in the rock, which supplied them with water. It is exceedingly interesting to observe that both these "cisterns to receive rain-water," and these "steps," are specially noted in connection with all the towers described by Josephus as standing upon the three walls.[1] In one place a ditch, some twenty feet wide, was found, with a rough rock slope below. On the western side were found at the foot of the scarp a number of fallen stones from three to four feet long, "many of which," says Lieutenant Conder, "seem to me to be Roman work, with a draft of three inches broad." He adds:[2] "The stones were found principally face downwards, as though fallen

---

[1] Josephus' *Wars of the Jews*, book v. chap. iv. sec. 3.

[2] See paper by Lieutenant Conder, R.E., in January *Quarterly Statement of Palestine Exploration Fund*, p. 7, and April *Quarterly Statement*, p. 18. This deeply interesting discovery has not yet received the attention it deserves.

from the tower above, or pushed over from within."
Here, then, in this modern glimpse at the famed
fortress of Jebus, we see rock-cut faces rising perpendicularly in one place to the height of perhaps
more than fifty feet. Well might David, rejoicing
in the security of God's people, allude in enthusiastic
language to these remarkable features as fitting
symbols of the Divine protection, and to the awe
with which they struck the minds of those monarchs
who came to besiege the city when they first beheld
them—

"Beautiful for elevation, the joy of the whole
    earth,
Is Mount Zion, on the sides of the north ;
The city of the great king.

   .   .   .   .

For lo, the kings were assembled,
They marched on together.
They beheld, and so they marvelled,
They were troubled, they hasted away ;
Trembling took hold upon them there,
Pain, as of a woman in travail.

   .   .   .   .

Walk about Zion, and go round about her,
Count her towers ;
Mark ye well her bulwarks.

   .   .   .   .

For this God is our God for ever and ever,
He will himself be our guide until [or, over]
    death."[1]

---

[1] Psalm xlviii. 2, 4-6, 12-14. The word I have translated
" elevation," נוֹף, *noaph*, only occurs in this place. It is evidently

Undoubtedly the rock face I have described must have formed part of the adamantine foundations upon which afterwards rose the first or old wall. Once huge ramparts crowned this scarp, and on the square projecting bases Herod built massive towers of immense strength. No stone of these can now be pointed out. Lieutenant Conder, reviewing Mr. Maudslay's important exploration, says it is especially "valuable as showing that, however the masonry may have been destroyed and lost, we may yet hope to find indications of the ancient enceinte *in the rock scarps which are imperishable.*" This is very true; for, while man can destroy what man has made, the everlasting hills smile at his rage. Yet who can hear of it without perceiving the force and sublimity of that glorious description of the immobility of believers—

> " They that trust in Jehovah are as Mount Zion,
>   Which shall not be moved, it abideth for ever."

---

derived from נוף, *nooph,* which has the sense of " to lift up," and hence, in a technical sense, "to wave," "to lift up and wave to and fro," a wave-offering, which is its meaning in twenty places. Five times it has the sense of "lifting up and striking with," as of a sickle or a tool (Exodus xx. 25 ; Deuteronomy xxiii. 25, xxvii. 5 ; Joshua viii. 31 ; Isaiah x. 15), and seven times of "lifting up and shaking the hand in a threatening manner" (Isaiah x. 32, xi. 15, xiii. 2, xix. 16; Zechariah ii. 9; Job xxxi. 21). The word here, therefore, is a very suggestive one, and seems to convey the idea, not only of an elevated place, lifted up on high, and offered as it were to God, but of one that defies its foes.

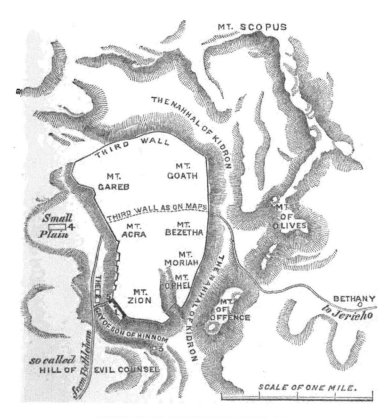

SKETCH MAP OF JERUSALEM AND ITS ENVIRONS.

1. The Protestant Cemetery, the black line to the north-east of it showing
   the position of the scarped foundation of the wall of Zion.
2. *Birket es Sultan,* or Sultan's Pool.
3. The traditional Aceldama.
4. *Birket Mamilla.*
5. The School of the late Anglican Bishop.

T

Not less impressive is the comparison used to set forth their eternal security as safe-guarded by Jehovah Himself—

"The mountains are round about Jerusalem ;
And Jehovah is round about his people,
Henceforth, even for evermore."

The Holy City, on its seven closely-clustered but well-defined hills, is surrounded by deep narrow valleys, which make the ascent to the gates toilsome on every side but the north-west. Though the slopes ascending to the city on all sides are still steep, recent explorations have shown that in former times they were far more precipitous. The *débris* of the twenty-seven-times-sacked city lies upon them in one spot to the depth of 125 feet.[1] There now exists in England a deeply-interesting model of Jerusalem and its environs, exhibited by the Palestine Exploration Fund in the Science and Art Department of the South Kensington Museum. This model gives us the true ancient lie of the ground in and around the city, being an embossed copy of the rock contours, made accurately to scale, the result of years of scientific survey and exploration, embodying the careful work of Col. Sir Charles Wilson, R.E., Col. Warren,

[1] See *The Recovery of Jerusalem*, p. 187. A brief account of its twenty-seven sieges is given in *Our Work on Palestine* (Messrs. Bentley & Sons), pp. 48-66.

R.E., Lieut. Conder, R.E., Mr. Schick of Jerusalem, and others. Here we look upon the true
site of the city of David and Solomon, as it must
have existed before its deep ravines and abrupt
slopes were to a great extent buried and oblite-
rated, as they are now, under vast heaps of rubbish. No engineer can glance at this model and
doubt for a moment where the third or outer wall
of the city must have stood, namely, on the brow
of the natural ridge that runs, with a more or less
steep descent, all round the city, except for some
six hundred yards on the north-west. Now let any
one follow with a measure this brow of the ridge,
and he will find that it gives a circumference of four
miles, just the thirty-three stadia that Josephus
assigns to the outside limits of the city![1] It is
strange that any doubt should ever have existed
on this point, and yet in very few plans of the
city is this line suggested.

If we bear in mind the position thus assigned, it
adds much force to the figure under consideration.
Jerusalem in ancient times was not only "beautiful
for elevation," but also secure and strong, beyond
most cities, on the same account. With its massive
and lofty walls, resting for the greater part of four
miles on the brow of rocky precipitous hills, it was

[1] "The whole compass of the city was thirty-three furlongs."—
Josephus, *Wars of the Jews*, book v. chapter iv. section 3.

entirely surrounded, except for a few hundred yards, by the *nahhal*, or torrent valley, of Kidron, on the north and east, and the *gay*, or ravine-like glen, of the son of Hinnom, or Gehenna, on the west and south. Beyond these rise the mountain of Scopus on the north, from which may be had the finest view of the city, and the Mount of Olivet on the east, which is a continuation of Scopus, where it turns abruptly to the south. Olivet, after running for about three-quarters of a mile, slightly dips, and rises again in a separate hill called the Mount of Offence, where the village of Siloam, now *Silwan*, still clings to its steep sides, and where once upon its summit, towering high above the sanctuary of Jehovah, the idol temple of Solomon's heathen wives commanded the Holy City. The narrow vale of Gehenna along the west and south, one of the most verdant and picturesque in all the neighbourhood, is shut in by the present so-called Hill of Evil Counsel, a terraced ridge with bold limestone cliffs, honeycombed by excavated sepulchres, which in some parts rises to a considerable elevation. The mountains most emphatically stand "round about Jerusalem," and in doing so must have greatly safeguarded it in ancient times. We are specially told that when Titus besieged the city, he found it impossible to invest it completely until he had built a wall round the entire sides of these mountains, nearly five miles long, with thirteen places at intervals in which he

stationed garrisons, which added another mile and a
quarter to these vast earthworks. "The whole was
completed," says the Jewish historian, "in three
days; so that what would naturally have required
some months was done in so short an interval as is
incredible."[1] Assaults upon the city, even then, could
only be delivered effectively upon its level corner
to the north-west, whence every hostile advance
was necessarily directed in all its various sieges.
To those familiar with these facts, beautifully bold,
graphic, and forceful is the Psalmist's figure of the
security of the Lord's people—

> " The mountains are round about Jerusalem ;
> And Jehovah is round about his people,
> Henceforth, even for evermore."[2]

---

[1] Josephus, *Wars of the Jews*, book v. chap. xii. section 2.

[2] To some, accustomed to our use of the word "mountains," it
has seemed that hills like Scopus, Olivet, the Mount of Offence,
&c., closely clustering round the Holy City, are not lofty or large
enough to be dignified with such a title, and these have been led to
look for "the mountains round about Jerusalem" in the peak of
Neby Samwil, some three and a half miles away, in the grand natural
wall of Moab, rising up to a height of over 4000 feet from the
Jordan valley, at a distance of 25 miles, and some other far-off but
conspicuous elevations. We must, however, remember that the
term רַה, *har*, "mountain," is given in Scripture to any comparatively large ridge, or collection of small hills, and to many such a
hogs-back as Scopus or Olivet. The hill over Jericho, the modern
Ain es Sultan, is called a *har*, or "mountain" (Joshua ii. 16). Ebal
and Gerizim are each called a *har* (Deuteronomy xi. 29) ; Zion,
which is overlooked by most of the hills which I have described as
standing round it, is repeatedly spoken of as a *har* (2 Kings xix. 31 ;

These words must have sounded in Hebrew ears as sublime as they were comforting, and, when sung on the heights of Zion, inspiring in the last degree.

Jerusalem may indeed fitly stand as an image of the believing and ever-tried people of God. Its history, like that of the Church militant, has been one of continual warfare. It has been well remarked by Mr. Grove, in summing up the annals of the city, that while our first glimpse of it in the Old Testament tells how the children of Judah "smote it with the edge of the sword, and set the city on fire," so "almost the latest mention of it in the New Testament is contained in the solemn warnings in which Christ foretold how Jerusalem should be compassed with armies." [1]   Twenty-seven times the waves of wild Eastern war have beaten upon its embattled walls. It has a story of trial and suffering without a parallel in the history of

Psalm ii. 6, &c.) ; and Olivet itself is in one place actually called by this name (Zechariah xiv. 4). There can be, therefore, no doubt of the appropriateness and literal accuracy of speaking of Jerusalem as surrounded by "mountains" in the case of the hills in close proximity to its walls. These mountains, with their deep intervening glens, stand like vast earthworks and fosses—a natural fortification—around the Holy City. Distant heights both afford no marked protection to Zion, and fail to convey any sense of that nearness and immediatecy of the Divine presence and power which the Psalmist seems to be expressing.

[1] Judges i. 8 ; Luke xxi. 20. See article on Jerusalem in Smith's *Bible Dictionary.*

any other spot. Yet it still remains a city of some thirty thousand inhabitants, surrounded by lofty and picturesque walls, and we know from the prophetic word that it is finally to enjoy a never-ending future of peace and glory. But before the arrival of this happy time a last terrible trial of unexampled severity awaits Jerusalem, namely, that foretold by our Saviour, and plainly predicted in so many passages of the prophets.[1] The Jewish population of the city has doubled in recent years, and events now rapidly ripening are preparing the way for Israel's return to the Holy Land as a nation, while yet in unbelief. This temporary solution of the Eastern Question is to be looked for at any moment. But what will happen when God, thus working by the political necessities of the times, causes them to return to the land that He gave to their fathers ? Let Jeremiah answer—

> " Alas ! for that day is great,
> So that none is like it :
> It is even the time of Jacob's trouble." [2]

Daniel, speaking of " the time of the end," when he represents Israel as seen in their own land, suffering a fearful and overwhelming invasion at the hands of the King of the North, declares of that

---

[1] Matthew xxiv. ; Luke xxi. ; Isaiah li. 17–23 ; lix. 1–18 ; Ezekiel xx. 32—xxi. 27 ; Joel ii. ; Zephaniah i.

[2] Jeremiah xxx. 3–7.

siege of Jerusalem, " there shall be a time of distress, such as never was since there was a nation even to that same time." [1] Zechariah, foretelling the closing scenes of this dispensation, as we learn from the following verses, says in the name of the Lord, " I will gather all the nations against Jerusalem to battle; and the city shall be taken, and the houses rifled, and the women ravished; and half of the city shall go forth into captivity." [2]

To quote from the author's *Palestine Repeopled.* " In the twenty-second chapter of Ezekiel, we have a dark picture of Israel's impiety, followed by a threatening of their long dispersion : ' I will scatter thee among the heathen, and disperse thee in the countries, and will consume thy filthiness out of thee !' But even this long discipline will not be sufficient, therefore we read in the following verses :— ' Because ye all become dross, behold, therefore, I will gather you into the midst of Jerusalem. As they gather silver, and copper, and iron, and lead, and tin, into the midst of the furnace, to blow the fire upon it, to melt it, so will I gather you in mine anger and in my fury, and I will lay you on, and melt you. Yea, I will gather you, and blow upon you in the fire of my wrath, and ye shall be melted in the midst thereof. As silver is melted in the midst of the furnace, so shall ye be melted in the midst

---

[1] Daniel xii. 1. [2] Zechariah xiv. 2.

thereof. And ye shall know that I, Jehovah, have poured out my fury upon you.'"[1] These terrible final judgments are to be correctional. The Lord "doth not willingly afflict and grieve the children of men," and in the issue we learn that the coming sorrows of the Jewish people are to be blessed of God to their conversion, and their restoration to the Divine favour. In view, however, of this time of Jacob's trouble, the last and worst of eighteen centuries of suffering, it will be seen at once how these very mountains, which served to make Jerusalem secure before the days of cannon, will only add so many new terrors to the siege of the future !

[1] Ezekiel xxii. 19–22.

INDEX OF HEBREW WORDS

EXPLAINED IN THIS WORK.

	PAGE		PAGE		PAGE
אוֹפָן	197	דּוּשׁ	233	מוֹץ	234
אַיָל	61	הַר	294	מוֹרַג	230
אֵל	170	חֶרֶב	85	מַטֶּה	158, 173
אֱלֹהִים	170	חָרוּץ	231	מֵישׁר	283
אָפְנִים	196	חַרְסוּת	120	מַשְׂכִּית	196
אָפִיק	59	חֹרֶף	78	מִשְׁעֶנֶת	272
אָפָק	59	חָרַף	78	מַתְבֵּן	241
בְּאֵר	113	חָרַץ	232	נָאַץ	93
בְּמוֹ	241	חֶרֶשׁ	120	נוּף	288
בָּנָה	226	טַל	136	נוֹף	287
בַּקְבֻּק	120	טָלַל	136	נָזַל	141
בִּקְעָה	264	טְלַל	136	נָחַל	264
בְּרֶךְ	115	יְאֹר	205	נָטָה	159
בְּרָכָה	115	יֶלֶד	147	נָטַר	211
גֶּדֶר	53	יַלְדוּת	147	נֹמֶר	211
גָּדַר	53	יָתֵד	8	נָצַר	211
גְּדֵרָה	53	לֶחֶם	70	נֹצֵר	211
גַּיְא	264	מַדְמֵנָה	241	סְאָה	33
גֹּרֶן	228, 229	מוֹאָב	241	עֹז	173

INDEX OF SCRIPTURE REFERENCES.

U

INDEX OF SUBJECTS.

Names of Hebrew, Arabic, Greek, and Latin words, Names of Arabic Towns, and Titles of Books, are in italics.

THE END.

PRINTED BY BALLANTYNE, HANSON AND CO.
EDINBURGH AND LONDON

Lightning Source UK Ltd.
Milton Keynes UK
UKHW020843230822
407709UK00006B/491